Emma,

The T .p

Chatham to Calcutta
Overland
Sept-Oct 1950

Iain Radford

ISBN 1-904499-10-4

First published in United Kingdom of Great Britain in 2006 by Roundtuit Publishing, 32 Cookes Wood, Broompark, Durham DH7 7RL

Printed in the United Kingdom of Great Britain by Prontaprint Durham

Contents

Iain*, Jim & Shaw with Haigh. C. Gulstain (the Ankara agent in Teheran)

*Also known as Ron or Ronnie

Preface

This is the day to day record of an overland journey from Chatham to Calcutta, and beyond, undertaken in 1950 by three young Sapper officers, Captains Jim and Iain Radford and Shaw McCloghry. The only remarkable things about the trip were, firstly, nobody, as far as we could tell, had attempted the journey since before the war and it was probably another six or seven years before anyone repeated it, and, secondly, there was not a war going on anywhere along the route. There were, however, considerable doubts about whether we should get permission to enter Yugoslavia. Although Tito had broken with, and was being blockaded by, the USSR, Yugoslavia was to all intents and purposes a closed country, still being a Communist state and deeply suspicious of the West. Our destination was Calcutta, as civil war in Northern Burma meant that entry permits were not even worth applying for, and, in any case, the roads, or rather tracks, were said to be impassable.

The idea was mine. Shaw I had known since we were both at Wellington. We had joined up on the same day, gone out to India on the same troopship and been commissioned together into the Royal Engineers, to serve in Queen Victoria's Own Madras Sappers and Miners. My brother, Jim, another 'Madras Sapper', was, at twenty-nine, the old man of the party. Knowing that, after a year in this country, he was fed up with soldiering in Britain and would welcome a chance to get back out East, I recruited him by writing to him of the plan and saying that, unless I heard from him within a week, I was putting his name forward to the War Office as one of the team.

Jim, who incidentally did not reply, combined an almost oriental calm and patience, which at times he certainly needed, with considerable skill with vehicles and a prodigious appetite for beer. He was the leader of the expedition, and a bachelor. Shaw was slight and dark, thin of face and hair, his life divided between periods of intense activity and supine idleness. Shaw and I were both about twenty four and had both married while we were waiting for the War Office to approve the trip, as we did not expect to be back in UK for another three years. Although all three of us were Sappers, none of us were Methodist or madder than one would expect.

Our vehicle was a 2 ton, two wheel drive, civilian, Austin truck, which we bought with the aid of my parents. It had a bench seat in front that took the three of us, and the back fitted up for sleeping, with three iron bunks, a rack of 'jerry cans' for water and petrol, two huge lockers for supplies and spares, including half-shafts and springs, and sand mats in case of trouble in the desert. The back was boxed in with an 'expanded metal' wire cage, for security, wire mosquito mesh and boasted a back door, while the canvas covers at the sides could be rolled up, at night, for air. Cooking was on a petrol-fuelled two burner stove and toilet arrangements a jerrycan of water, an aluminium basin and a spade.

The War Office obligingly arranged for all three of us to be posted back to the Far East, granted us the cost of a troopship passage to Singapore and allowed us to add the passage time to our annual leave. This gave us exactly eight weeks on full pay; any time after that and we would forfeit both pay and seniority, a serious disincentive to dawdling. In return, they invited us to report on the state of the roads on our way and lent us a superior camera, which, when we reached Calcutta, we found did not work. Consequently, we have no photos of the trip.

The rest of this account (apart from the comments in italics, many copied from a letter I wrote in 1951) is extracted from a carbon record of the less personal parts of almost daily letters to Jane, my bride of three months, who later joined me in Hong Kong; the last I had seen of her was on the dockside at Dover, where we had loaded the truck onto the ferry for Calais. The final letter was to my father.

Part One: Chatham to Macedonia

Letter 1   *Near St Dizier, 1ˢᵗ Sept 1950*

My darling Jane ....The first thing we did on board was to head for the bar, where we had a duty-free beer and bought a thousand cigarettes. We then said good-bye to the white cliffs of Dover, had another beer, and consigned a particularly insanitary object that Jim described as his hairbrush, to Father Neptune, who ignored it. It wouldn't have been any use to a bald mermaid!

We landed at dusk and set off into France, following the notice boards saying 'Toutes Directions'. When these stopped we asked a very surprised Frenchman, in our best and almost forgotten school French, the way to Dijon, which we imagined was our first port of call in France. Unfortunately, it is somewhere in the deep South and we had to hurriedly get out a map and ask for somewhere nearer.

The roads were terrible, all cobbled and wet and going in no particular direction, and as soon as we were well clear of the town we picked a spot to sleep and just parked the truck at the side of the road. We went to bed chewing apples as we had no water to wash with *(We could not fill our petrol cans in England because of petrol rationing and assumed that our water cans were also empty)* and soon began to regret our choice of campsite. We seemed to have picked the major sewer in north France to camp by, though we blamed Jim's feet, *which stuck out at the end of his bunk,* and vast lorries rumbled past us all night. There was a puddle outside the back door and a train passed within a few yards of us. It turned out that we were still in the town and surrounded on three sides by canals and the fourth by a railway.

France

After that we bashed on fairly uneventfully, except when Jim
forgot on which side of the road to drive while looking for
breakfast and a place to shave and other things. There did not
seem to be a decent sized hedge for fifty miles. However we
finally got to Lille and decided on breakfast, which was bread,
butter, rhubarb jam and coffee. Quite good coffee, but oddly
enough, each cup had its own little percolator on top. Thirty
francs a cup for black coffee - we drank beer for the rest of the
day. Lunch we had at St Quentin, after taking a photo of the
truck with the cathedral in the background. We had an
enormous mushroom omelette, wine and Gruyere cheese -
delicious. *After driving all day through fine farm country,* we
stopped here at about six after picking up petrol, bread ["How
much, Monsieur?" " So much" - about a yard, which she cut
off and weighed], fresh butter and more marvellous fresh
Gruyere. Before supper we boiled up some water and
washed. It turned out that our water cans had been full all the
time with rusty water. (*We soon learned to wash all over with a
small amount of hot water in the ally basin.*)

Then I walked off up the road to find a farm and summoning
up all my schoolboy French - which came back very quickly - I
asked for some milk, which was fetched direct from the
cowshed, and I walked back to the truck swinging the pot like
a farmer's girl! Supper of fried eggs on bread and butter -
thick butter - washed down with fresh milk. A meal fit for a
king. Now the other two are playing a game of patience called
`bitched, bothered and bewildered', and I am thinking of bed.

Letter 2   *Near Lyons, France, 2nd Sept*

My darling Jane, this morning we got off to an early start; up at about six, when the first one woke. *Having changed our minds about growing beards, which felt too dirty for words,* Jim and Shaw shaved, so did I as a matter of fact, but it was not such a notable matter, for they had looked like tramps all day. We are keeping our white overalls for working on the truck or triumphal entries, I am not sure yet which, so our clothes are a bit mixed: Jim in red sweat rag, windcheater and khaki drill slacks and chaplies *(sandals)* on his feet; Shaw in a blue Indian shirt, a pair of khaki SD trousers of his father's, and an army web belt; and yours truly in blue shirt, blue cords and a red rag round my neck with horses on it - also chaplies. This rigout has its advantages besides comfort, for when we ask for a restaurant we are directed to the cheapest, where the food is just as good. Talking of food, we lunched off little French melons and tomatoes prepared with vinegar and oil, followed by delicious steak and beans - Darling you must come to France and learn how to cook beans - and pears; all washed down with beautiful red wine, no label on the bottle, of course, but better than anything I have ever tasted in the Mess. The only trouble was that we had no idea when a course started or how or in what order to eat. This was at Dijon.

I trust that the French will forgive us for remembering nothing of their beautiful country but the marvellous food. We had, however, just come from rationed England.

After lunch we had a spot of excitement when, coming down a steep hill into a narrow village street with a right angle bend in it, Shaw inadvertently put his foot on the accelerator instead of the brake, *(while trying to change into low gear)* and we scattered the crowd on the pavement. However no harm was done, and all was well until we met a herd of cows, *which being even more frightened than us, scattered just in time* – after that Jim made Shaw put his foot straight on the brake pedal as soon as he took it off the accelerator. (*My memory of careering down the narrow road between the high banks, grimly hauling on the hand brake, is so vivid that, until I re-read the journal, I thought I was the driver! This reflects the fact that both Shaw and I were really very inexperienced drivers. We must have been a sore trial to Jim!*)

The truck is a honey and goes along quite happily at 40 mph, which *Jim keeps us to and* we hope is the economical speed, but she has lots in reserve. The only thing worrying us a little is the petrol consumption, which seems a bit high – but of course we are stymied by the fact that we buy petrol in litres and the distances are in kilometres, so it may be better than we think. Prices are terrible; food is no cheaper than at home, wine of any named variety is about the same, while petrol is about half as expensive again, *but unrationed!*

We came through Lyons this evening, which is about the best town we have seen so far. We had followed a river all day, and thought it must be the Rhône. Jim took a beautiful picture of a bridge across it. Imagine our surprise, therefore, when, when we asked the way to Grenoble, we were told to go over the second bridge, straight on through the place, and turn right when we came to the Rhône, and go over the fourth bridge. Jim didn't believe our interpretation, but sure enough the second bridge was twice as big as the first.

We came to our first vineyards today – most unimpressing, not even as big as good blackberry bushes – growing on low wires *instead of the hop-poles we had expected,* with little bunches of small grapes. And what is more, no wall *nor tower.* I had always imagined a vineyard to be like a backyard, after all I am sure that the king in the parable builded a wall around his vineyard and built a tower before departing to a far country.

However the vines were an improvement on the everlasting strip cultivation we had been passing.

We bathed tonight in hot water and washed up in it too.... very luxurious. The stove is a marvel and quite puts any primus to shame. Supper of half a yard of bread, butter and sausages with a couple of pints of tea each. The truck is looking very tidy inside, now that we have got everything stowed away and the hooks up.

Letter 3   *30 km before Turin, Italy, 3ʳᵈ Sept*

My Darling, we decided on an early start today and got up at 5.30 and were on the move by 7.00 o'clock, consequently we made good speed and have almost reached Turin. We came over the Cenis Pass between Grenoble and Susa about midday, stopping for lunch at St Michele. We had pate-de-fois and gherkins, followed by a huge plate of rice done with tomatoes, then melon, then steak and mushrooms and finished with pears. The wine was good too. *Note: - I suspect that this obsession with food reflects not only our youth but the fact that food in England was still rationed.*

The country had been getting a little like the Downs instead of being quite flat, but the Alps were a complete surprise, rising out of the countryside in a series of huge buttresses and pinnacles, and as we drove up the valley, bigger and bigger peaks appeared round each corner until they were snow covered *or, to be more exact, each dignified pate wore a little toupee of snow*. The road, however, was remarkably good, dead straight for miles on end, though rising steadily until the last few miles where we climbed up in a series of bights, loops and hairpins, and wound through great pine forests, patched with snow, with little castles on the peaks frowning down on us. All the same it was a good surface and well cambered and we got to the top in third gear, *passing lots of cars on the way,* though admittedly she boiled a bit. Then we set off down the hill again and soon our engine temperature was right down and the paint was burning off the brake drums.

The Italian Customs were a huge joke, gathering around and chattering about our trip; all dressed in beautiful uniforms, slightly frayed, and beards. *Note:- They were intrigued with the RE, AA and Madras S&M badges on the truck, and were convinced that the RE badge, which sported wings, must be RAF. We settled for RAF Engineers.* The only thing they took exception to was our stock of cigarettes. Apparently, instead of the 500 a head we were allowed in France, we could only bring 200 a head into Italy. We gave them 80 and everyone was happy. They didn't look at anything else.

Italy is a shocking country. The roads have little surface and the people and the houses look like something out of the East. The only thing they seem to have plenty of is a type of motor scooter, very nicely designed and good looking, with the engine in a bulge alongside the back wheel. They always seem to carry two people, whether grandpa with a beard and grandma or granddaughter of about seven, or, more frequently, a young fellow in a sweater and a girl with beautiful long sunburnt legs *riding side-saddle* – we sat in a cafe drinking beer and watching the legs for a long time. The beer was not very good.

We found a promising looking side turning and went up it to find a campsite at about half past five, and found a man with a gun, who spoke no word of any language we knew but said we could camp here. Asking him where we could get milk was more difficult; I pointed at a cow, while Shaw mooed; He thought we wanted it moved. I made drinking motions, *while Jim laughed*, and he thought we wanted beer, Chianti and water, in that order. Finally I made milking movements beside the cow and he twigged at once. He called over a woman working in a hayfield and they milked the cow straight into our milk jug!

Letter 4   *Montebello, Italy, 4th Sept*

My darling Jane…… We left our camp this morning at seven and after a short run over reasonable roads reached Turin. We came onto the famous Autostrada and had to pay a tax of 500 lire to ride on it – this is not as bad as it sounds being only about 6/-. but it was worth it, for although the road was not very wide, it was dead straight, well surfaced and flew over every crossroads for 100 miles. *There were, as yet, no motorways in England.* Bicycles and carts were not permitted on it, and consequently we bashed on at forty miles an hour the whole way. The only two turnings on the whole road were one at Milan and one at Bergamo, where side roads came in. *Its only disadvantage was that it studiously avoided all hills or picturesque villages, so it is not the route to take if your object is to see Italy.*

We made a detour at Milano in order to look up the ancestors – it is a fine city and the cathedral or Duomo is huge and gothic, lighted only by the dim light through the glowing stained glass windows – very impressive. *I was refused entry to the Duomo until I changed out of the shorts I was wearing.* Unfortunately I got mixed up with a crowd of tourists or pilgrims and went to have a look at somebody's tomb. There I was politely stopped and asked for alms in English, but Jim is our treasurer and since he and Shaw were sitting outside drinking Chianti, I had not a cent. I had driven into the middle of the town, just to prove I could, but I was quite happy to let Jim drive out again. It is a big city and oddly enough I had driven straight to the Duomo, a very complicated route, entirely by hereditary instinct! I wanted to look at the castle on the way out but Jim maintained that we had wasted enough time already. *Jim and Shaw had about as much interest in sightseeing as Goths. Given my way we should never have finished the trip on time!* We lunched off fried veal cutlets, gorgonzola and pears – good but not quite up to the French meals – at Bergamo. Later we stopped to fill up with petrol and top up our water cans, and found that the Yale lock on the back door would not answer to the key. Eventually we levered the door open with wedges and screwdrivers, but it was very annoying. Jim, I think has fixed it while I was starting to cook supper, and I hope it will be all right from now on.

Jim and Shaw are most indignant at the idea that they swilled Chianti while I was in the Duomo. They maintain that they just looked at the empty bottle!

Verona was a picturesque spot with battlements and walls of many ages, in concentric layers -- the inner like the tower of London, the middle like the Ravelin at Chatham and pill boxes outside. We stopped at Montebello for provisions and had a long argument in three languages as to whether a pile of stuff was butter or cheese. Finally we bought it and though it smelt like cheese, it tasted like butter. *We could buy no butter in Italy that did not smell rancid. None of the stalls or shops had refrigerators, and we had not twigged that we should have been using olive oil.* We also bought a couple of feet of bread and a half dozen eggs, and a bottle of white Chianti.

I seem to have assumed that Chianti was the generic name for all Italian wine. It was better than the red, for they gave us half a dozen glasses to choose from. *We had some difficulty trying to persuade them that we wanted to buy a flask not a glass, but all they did was pour out yet another glass for us to try. Eventually the vendor reached up onto a shelf and took down one of a line of splendidly labelled flasks.* It is a lovely bottle, all bound with straw and covered with labels, although we know it was filled from a barrel in the cellar, *with the wine we had chosen.* Rumble-tumble eggs for supper – very good.

The most noticeable thing about Italy, apart from the scooters and the Chianti seems to be the general prevalence of animal transport; most of the light carts are pulled by a mule, while either a couple of cows or bullocks pull the heavy wagons. France was lovely in this respect with beautiful horses – two to a cart, three to a plough or four to a wagon, they were a fine sight.

The other noticeable feature has been that every fifty yards for the past two hundred miles there has been a huge advertisement hoarding at the side of the road. Usually they are repeated half a dozen times in succession to rub it in, and some are thirty or forty foot hight... *(sic)...*. Excuse the spelling, Darling; we have just finished another bottle of Chianti. *The Autostrada was lined on both sides with these hoardings. The ones I remember were a vast Michelin man who straddled the Autostrada, and Olio Sasso lollipops which rose and fell like the waves of the sea, for a hundred yards at a time.*

	Olio		**Olio**	
Sasso		**Sasso**	**Sasso**	**Sasso**
Olio		**Olio**		**Olio**

Letter 5   *Trieste, 7th Sept*

My Darling Jane, Venice is the most beautiful spot I have ever seen, *where we sat among the pigeons outside St Mark's, sipping the gentlest fire ever trapped in a cocktail,* and of all the places I have been it is the one I really want to go back to. *We had expected a tangle of dirty canals and an odour of departed glory, and found instead a sunbathed city of incredible beauty.* The city is a glory of old houses, rising high out of the canals *and each with its reflection dancing attendance in the waters,* little humped-back bridges, winding lanes and huge squares and glorious churches. One day we will come here for a holiday, take a gondola and explore the place by moonlight, or spend all day in the warmest sunshine that I have met in Europe out on the Lido, and some days we will go shopping for the most exquisite glass and lace, leather and cameos and all the beautiful things they make or sell.

The lace is the loveliest I have ever seen, gorgeous parasols made of ivory and black lace, shawls and scarves and collars and all things lovely made of the white. While the glass surpassed even the lace in beauty - scarlet painted vases, fishes heads holding candlesticks and the loveliest of lovely figures, both of coloured glass speckled with gold inside and in porcelain.

I still remember a Negro jazz band, gold instruments, dusky figures with gold speckled harem trousers swaying to the tune they were playing. Price £50 when my pay was £30 a month.

As I said, Darling, forget any ideas you ever had of a holiday anywhere else. We are going to save up and come to Venice.

We arrived here *(Trieste, where there was still a British garrison deterring the Yugoslavs from seizing the city)* at about five thirty in the evening, and walked into the Adjutant's office. He said

`Good evening, could he do anything for us'? I replied that we were three Sapper officers on leave who wanted accommodation. Jim volunteered the fact that we were on our way to Calcutta, and Shaw put the lid on it by adding "Not Calcutta really, Singapore." This shook the poor man so severely that he asked to see our identity cards – after which we were welcomed to the Mess and given so much beer that I did not write to you that night.

We spent yesterday on a fairly hopeful search for our Yugoslav visas and our mail, but got neither. (We had had our passports visa'd for every country between France and India except Yugoslavia. The Yugoslav Embassy in London had told us visas would be waiting for us in Trieste). We hope to get the visa tomorrow, but have no idea of what has happened to the mail. Unfortunately there is no British Consul here and we are still hoping it will be sent to someone in the town, rather than to the nearest consul, who is 100 miles away in Venice.

In the evening one of the local Sappers and I went to the opera. It was a memorable experience. They have turned the keep of an old castle on the top of the town into an open-air opera house, and while we sat in the 6/- seats in the stalls, the 1/- seating or rather standing room was all round the battlements. It was a lovely setting, the place holding, I suppose, about five or six thousand, and the show was to match. It was a production by the local company of the Merry Widow. Dialogue and singing was all in Italian, and I still have not a clue what the plot was, but the music was good, the singing lovely – no microphones, just marvellous voices – and the dancing girls and the costumes....... but I suppose the less said the better. It was the first time I had seen a Can-can on a live stage. ....forty girls... phweh!

Letter 6   *Trieste (morning), 9th Sept*

My Darling Jane. We are still in Trieste but have good hopes of shifting this morning. The day before yesterday we were right down in the dumps. Our visas showed no sign of coming through. *The Yugoslav official we saw had a huge mahogany desk without a scrap of paper or even a telephone on it. He obviously had no authority to do anything but refer to Belgrade.* and when we went into the Italian Tourist agency to see about the second half of our Italian carnet form, the little man swore black and blue that the carnet was the wrong type for 'Yugland'. We cursed the AA and went out and had a drink. It is much recommended and called Cinzana __ it was a sort of vermouth and tasted like Cascara and ice (luckily it didn't have the same effect). Then we went along to the Yug Tourist Agency and they referred us to the Legation, so we went to bed thinking in terms of boats to Greece.

However yesterday the visa people were much more cheerful and told us the carnet would do, and at lunchtime when we rang up, they said they would visa our passports at 9.00 o'clock today, whether or not they got a confirmatory telegram from Belgrade.

The rest of the day it was like walking on air, and in the evening we went out to have an Italian meal. The local Trieste speciality is a risotto with scampi or prawns and shrimps. When we asked for this the waiter said it would take about half an hour to cook, and would we like an omelette first? We would. The Risotto was huge and delicious and we were settling back in our chairs finishing our wine and rubbing our tummies when the waiter asked us what we would like for the main course! We decided that Rosbeef a l'Anglais wasn't really a local dish and wanted game. For the next ten minutes we watched Shaw and the waiter cackling, crawing and flapping their arms in order to describe the various birds available. I was only hoping that one or the other would suggest Nightingale. However we plumped for Woodcock and very good they were, even when Jim produced the head and beak out of his helping and put it to use by eating the brain.

Letter 7   *On the banks of the Danube, Mon 11th Sept*

My Darling Jane. We have arrived at Belgrade now after getting our visas in Trieste the day before yesterday. They had been being B minded for a long time, but finally said that they had authorisation by phone from Belgrade and would let us have them next morning, whether they had the cable or not. The only snag we had was that when we reached the boundary of the Free Territory, *(Trieste was neither part of Italy nor Yugoslavia)* they sent us all the way back into Trieste to get our carnet cleared at the Central Customs House. The Yugs, on the other hand, were charming and very helpful and they have kept it up ever since. *(The attitude of individual Yugoslavs was in sharp contrast to that of Tito's officials).*

The difference of opinion between the British here and in Trieste about the Yugs is remarkable. In Trieste they all regarded them as a set of B minded thugs, whereas here everyone has a considerable liking and admiration for them. After all they had a very good record during '39-'45 and '14-'18 wars and before that against the Turks. They are a handsome, hospitable and charming race, and under the circumstances one cannot blame them for their government. Slivovitch is good stuff too; a very potent plum brandy. They also have a drink called Rukya, made by distilling the skins and pips of the grapes after they have been pressed for wine. The first time we came across this was yesterday on the road. We had given a bloke a lift for about forty five miles along the Autoput with a spare tyre and big end bearing for his lorry. *(The Autoput was a dead straight, concrete, single carriage way road all the way from Zagreb to Belgrade. As the Russians had cut off their supplies of petrol, the only vehicles we met in 100 miles were a couple of bullock carts and the one broken down truck, which turned out to be an ex-British army REME machinery lorry with the most remarkable kink in it where the halves of two different trucks had been inexpertly welded together)* His pals at once rallied round, sent off a boy to the nearest farm for a carafe of Rukya *(He departed at a run and returned driving a mule cart like Jehu)* and we had a party. They were all very pro-British and anti-government, and plied us with Balkan cigarettes while we drank the spirit. It was undiluted and rather like a mixture of arrack and liquid fire, but very good in the heat of the day. *(perhaps it was just as well we had the road to ourselves!)*. They were full of complaints against Tito *(thumbs down)*, and compliments for Churchill and Truman *(thumbs up)*.

The first day in the country, we crossed the border at about half past three and drove over shocking roads until about ten thirty at night. We had almost reached Zagreb. In the morning we played hide and seek with a cowherd and two cows while we hid in the bushes, ostensibly for a certain reason but actually trying to photograph quite a fine bridge (and an ancient steam locomotive). That day we were up at five o'clock, and bashed off down the new Autoput to Belgrade. (The newly finished Autoput is the showpiece of a five-year plan). A lovely drive, though the country got flat and a bit monotonous after the lovely hill scenery of the day before. I suppose it is the best road we have yet met, but very little traffic on it. Tito can build roads but cannot buy lorries to put on them.

When we arrived at the British Embassy here, we looked so dirty that the assistant-assistant Secretary took us in at the servants entrance and gave us a bath before doing anything else, but when we reappeared in respectable clothes, everyone we met was charming and we have had a lovely day waiting for our extension visa. Unfortunately, when we did eventually get our Yug visas (*in Trieste*), they were transit visas and only valid for two days.

Shaw is most unreasonably bucked by getting a letter, while Jim and I have not, but we are hoping for one at Salonika. (*Our mail was all addressed via British Embassies and Consulates along the way*).

(Letter continued, 12 September)

Yesterday afternoon, when I failed to finish this letter, we were bathing in the Sava, a mile or two above its confluence with the Danube. The water was pleasantly warm, the sun just right for sunbathing and the spot lovely. There were even some logs of rafts, or rather rafts of logs, on the bank which made lovely diving boards. It was a heavenly afternoon. (*This was a popular spot and our portable radio soon attracted a crowd. Tito did not permit private citizens to have radios which could listen to the BBC. I asked a group of young people whether the BBC attraction was the News, and was firmly told that it was not news but Jazz they wanted to hear.*)

After tea we went round and had drinks with the Ambassador, a charming old boy, and dined on our own. ... caviar, steak (with specially sharpened knives), mushrooms and rice - grapes in a bowl of iced water, and a lovely iced wine, rather like a Muscatel.

The prices of everything here are quite ridiculous, and I suppose we have spent forty or fifty pounds at the regular rate of exchange (*Note: A captains pay in UK was about £30 a month after tax*). Luckily we were told in Trieste that Dinars were cheap to buy there, so we bought five pounds worth and smuggled them in (*behind the reflectors of our headlights*). Here they were worth sixty.

After dinner we went off to a night club called the Lotus, a gloomy cellar with friezes and murals of ladies in various states of undress, quite a good band and most of the tables occupied by tie-less proletarians. The Communists here don't wear red ties. They wear none. I soon got bored, as the wine tasted like vinegar, and went off to bed, but I think Jim and Shaw stayed on for a cabaret.

(*Irrelevant Note: Years later in a nightclub in Nicosia where the main attraction was a very pretty dancer, I chivvied my companion, a communist UN official from Czechoslovakia, about patronising such 'bourgeois decadence'. His reply, gazing at the dancer, was 'O Yan.....But such delicious decadence!'*).

I take a dim view of night-clubs (*I wonder whether I had a hangover?*). We hope to be on the move by ten this morning, if our Visas are ready, and we are prepared for bad roads and worse heat all the way to Salonika, which we will make in two or three days.

I have a lovely chit here which describes me as

RONALD JAIN RADFORD, ENGLISKI

Letter 8   *Still in Belgrade, 12th Sept*

My darling Jane... We seem to be stuck here, though whether for two hours or two days we do not know.

Belgrade is an odd city. They are busy rebuilding all the bomb-blasted buildings, and they are building well; no house with less than five stories. Tito seems determined to have a modern capital. Unfortunately, though they can build these blocks, they cannot finish them off at once as there is a terrible shortage of plaster, plumbing, door knobs etc. A house may stand as an empty shell for a couple of years before they finish it. *We passed the skeletons of a new university which was built on sand and is slowly sinking. We were told that all the engineers responsible have been shot.*

The streets too are full of contrast. Handsome, fit, tough looking officers in beautiful uniforms, grey or fawn, rub shoulders with peasants in patched breeches and shaggy sheepskin or deerskin waistcoats, or black braided jackets, with little skullcaps and laced sandals with toes turned up a couple of inches in front, *and the huge limousines of the American Embassy hooting at gangs of political prisoners shambling off to work on yet another prestige project.*

The soldiers are a scruffy collection in dirty overalls, with next to no motor transport; but people here say they are trained as first class guerrillas.

The girls are pretty and the men a good looking bunch on the whole, but everyone is desperately poor. For instance you can sell a second hand suit for fifty pounds, while people in the Legation get their wine by buying bottles of Chianti in Trieste, and selling the empties here. They make money on it as well as getting their wine free. It would drive you to drink.

17

PS tell Max (*a family friend who ran all the tug boats on the Thames*) that he would like driving in this town; you do all your signalling by horn. When you meet a policeman (*There were more traffic police than cars*) it is one hoot for straight on, two to the right and three to turn left. If you want to turn round you keep your finger on the horn until you have finished the manoeuvre. (*As there were virtually no cars the streets were not unduly noisy, though it took us a while to find out what it was about our driving – no horn signals – that was making the traffic police so cross*).

Letter 9   *On the road to Nîs, 12ᵗʰ Sept*

Darling Jane

We have got our visas extended for another week, and left Belgrade at about three o'clock after paying our hotel bills, 1209 dinar, about ten pounds at the official rate for one double room for two nights. No meals on the establishment. (*Note: I think we thought this an outrageous price!*). Our friends at the Embassy ended by giving us a crate of beer to speed us on our way.

We have covered about eighty miles and are coming up into the hills, over roads that steadily get worse. The weather has stayed good and we hope to make good time tomorrow. Everyone here seems very pleasant and helpful, though of course we have no language in common.

I think I shall post this letter at the local post office tomorrow, so goodness knows when it will reach you. I suppose it will get through eventually.

I love you, my Darling, Give my love to Marmaduke (*alias Joanna, born the following year*) and look after him (*!*) well. Messages to everyone, Love Iain.

Part Two: Macedonia to Mosul

Letter 10 *Just short of Salonika, Greece, 14ᵗʰ Sept*

My darling Jane, we passed the Yugoslav frontier at about three o'clock this afternoon and are safely out from behind the Iron Curtain, with no worse loss than one driving mirror, pinched off the truck in Belgrade.

After we had got into Greece a mile or two, we met a 1920 Austin London Taxi, on its way home after a run down to Crete. It was occupied by three beards and two girls, whom the beards had picked up in Crete and were giving a lift home. We promptly had a party and erected a cairn (of empty beer bottles) to mark this historic event. The taxi's luggage compartment and roof were full of camping gear and haversacks, while the back seat was full of vegetables and similar local products. Luckily the taxi had a landau roof, and so four of the party sat on this with their feet on the back seat. They hadn't got a meter but their bill of rates was still intact.

We got away from Belgrade after lunch on Tuesday and have been going over roads that got steadily worse ever since until, here in Greece, some of the potholes have been three feet deep. Tito, at least, had a system of 'voluntary' labour for mending his roads, by which everyone in the country volunteers to do so many days or hours. The system is wasteful and the result far from perfect, but at least most of the potholes get filled up now and again, but Greece is a democracy and their roads are in bigger holes than my socks.

There has been a considerable contrast between the country and the people up North and those here. In the first areas we went through, (Croatia and Slovenia), the people wore

European clothes and little wayside shrines were much in evidence. These were, incidentally, well tended and decorated with flowers, while they actually grew dahlias in the cottage gardens.

Down South here we seemed to be right out of Europe. The peasant women in baggy trousers and the men in tip-turned sandals and fezzes or vast astrakhan hats, which with their beards make their faces look about two foot long; scarlet cummerbunds have been the order of the day and the standard transport for about two hundredweight of stores, one man or two women is a donkey.

We dropped in at the Consulate in Skoplje last night and gave the Consul the last of the apples *(from England)*. He retaliated with beer and cigarettes and as we wanted to use up the last of our Dinara, *(which were valueless outside the country)* we took him out to dinner. We had a lovely meal of kabobs, which is meat and bits and pieces fried on skewers and eaten with paprikas. We washed it down with a couple of litres of fierce rose-coloured wine, the first liquor we have drunk in this country that did not taste of plums.

We woke, as we had gone to bed, covered in about a quarter of an inch of dust. Every time we moved it a passing lorry threw in another layer. Consequently we were a little late starting for as soon as I got up I felt we had to have a cup of tea *(Was this because of the dust or the worst hangover anywhere on the trip?)* and everything else waited. However we were off by seven-fifteen (in a cloud of dust).

We stopped for lunch just short of the Yug frontier and hunted around for a cafe. The first we found was for officers only, but a charming bloke led us along to another, where the beer was served in pint tankards and the populace ate baked beans and brown bread while playing chess. However they did us better than the populace by giving us, first a vegetable and macaroni soup and then a dish of paprikas and liver in tomato sauce - delicious. Our object was to finish our Dinars, which are quite valueless outside the country, but since, at our private rate of exchange (*see earlier note about smuggling in headlamps*) a pint of beer cost tuppence halfpenny (official rate half a crown) we just could not do it.

The Yugs gave us our first really good customs search on the way out and Max's dollar notes came to light – we had to act very stupid to get away with them, for we had not declared them on entry.

The Yug -Greek frontier is a formidable affair of barbed wire with pill-boxes sat about half a mile back from it; consequently it was a long job getting through, for a Yug soldier had to escort us to the barrier and then wait until a Greek woke up and walked down from his hill top. Then the barrier was solemnly lifted by both of them and Jim drove through. The Greek wanted a lift back to the customs shed, and I had the odd experience of disarming our escort, for I was blowed if he was getting into the wagon with a loaded and cocked sten gun. We travelled four in the front with Shaw holding the mag and I the gun.

(*The roads in Northern Greece were much worse than in Yugoslavia. There they were reasonably well maintained gravel roads with only moderate potholes. In Greece they had been tarmaced once upon a time but the potholes were huge. Although it was getting dark, we pressed on as we thought it unwise to halt too close to the frontier.*)

Suddenly Jim, who was driving, slammed on the brakes and asked me to have a look at the next pothole. I jumped out and replied that it was six feet deep, and no pothole but a collapsed culvert. We managed to edge round the hole, but were a little apprehensive about mines.

Shortly afterwards our headlights picked up a couple strolling arm in arm down the road, then another and another, all in spotless shirts or dresses, which put our dusty selves to shame. As we approached the village, we realised that the entire population, in couples, dozens or scores were enjoying an evening stroll. The scene, lit only by a few lamps in the cottages, was rather like a crowd scene in a musical. Soon after we passed the village, I think, we stopped for the night)

We had a very pleasant surprise just now, for a Greek has come up to the truck, when we were cooking dinner and given us five pounds of lovely grapes. To judge from his gestures the British army shot some enemy of his and he has never repaid the debt.

Letter 11   *On the shores of the Aegean Sea, near Adrianoupolis, 16ᵗʰ Sept*

My darling Jane... We are camped tonight in a quiet bay on the sea shore, and can hear the water of the Aegean almost splashing the side of the truck. We had been looking forward to getting to the sea all day, and when we stopped Shaw and I whipped off our clothes and jumped in. A quiet bathe soon developed into a rag and we got all our towels wet and threw each others clothes into the sea, until the only dry things we had were our bathing costumes which we had not bothered to put on. Jim got a lovely snap entitled *Sunset over the Aegean* showing Shaw just entering the water! (*Like all our photos, this one was hopelessly out of focus. I seem to remember Shaw remonstrating that Jim might have waited until he was in a few inches deeper.*)

We got into Salonika early yesterday and went to see the Consul about mail and other things. To our disappointment, Consuls outside the Iron Curtain are not like those inside, so we got a rather frosty reception. However, as always our luck was in and we found the Military Attaché, Major Sedgewick. He entertained us royally on beer, beer and more beer and sent us off to lunch with a very good impression of Salonika. For lunch we had fried mussels and quail, both delicious, but could not find any squids, which we wanted to sample.

We then went off over pretty good roads, built with American aid, until we reached a pleasant spot near Serrai, where they had built a new bridge. (*Almost all the bridges in Northern Greece seemed to have been destroyed and replaced with Bailey or other temporary structures. I remember one stream we crossed spanned by a broken stone arch, a wrecked Bailey bridge and an improvised bridge.*) We hoped to be able to bathe and wash the truck down in the river. There was an additional advantage in the camp-site too, for there was a Greek Army piquet on the bridge, and as there are rumoured to be bandits about, we were quite glad of their company. When Jim and I were all ready to produce supper, we missed Shaw and ran him to ground in the Guard Room, where he was having a long chat with the guards, none of whom spoke any known language.

They invited us to sup with them, so we used our boiling water to make a lot of coffee and took it along with us. Later we also fetched the wireless and the rest of the grapes we had been given the evening before. The soldier's food consisted of whole fried fish, which they had caught in the river with hand grenades, a mixture of onions and tomatoes floating in olive oil and huge hunks of brown bread. Each man had his own bit of bread, but there were no plates, and the bowls of fish and tomatoes were free for all. We were a little stymied at first as to how to eat the fish, which were about six inches long. *(The Greeks would not start until we had, so we could not copy them.)* Jim preferred holding them by the head and eating the tail first, *(but judging from his expression, this did not seem a good idea)*, but I maintained that the head tasted better and started that end. *(I do not think this is a strictly true account. I must have been sparing Jane the details. I seem to remember that it was Shaw who tried biting the head, but I, being a clever beggar, picked mine up by both ends...... and got a mouthful of guts. The fish had not been cleaned, which did not worry our hosts who ate them whole.)*

We were interrupted, when we got to the cigarette stage, by the arrival of an officer *(with an escort of much more military looking soldiery. I suspect the first lot were a sort of Home Guard)*, who made us up-ship and off to Serai. *We protested that we wished to stay put for the night, but he would not take 'no' for an answer. Although he was quite polite, it was obvious that we were under arrest, although we showed him our passports and visas for Greece. We were allowed to travel in our own truck, but were escorted by armed guards and taken to the barracks,* where he produced an interpreter. *After questioning and a close examination of our papers,* he explained that the area round the bridge was out of bounds, for the bandits still like blowing up that sort of thing. *(We gathered that the Home Guard thought that we were Bulgarian saboteurs bent on demolishing the bridge they were guarding, but instead of arresting us straight off, had brought us into their Guard Room where they could keep an eye on us until reinforcements arrived)* So we slept the night on the barrack square, and overslept shamefully into the bargain, not waking up until half past six.

Since then I have always felt vaguely apprehensive about travelling in Greece in case I might still be mistaken for a Bulgarian saboteur.

Today the good road turned bad and then worse & we rattled and jolted along for most of the time. The scenery was varied though, sometimes barren hills, *the home of lots of tortoises*, and now and again fertile irrigated valleys, and everywhere little towns clinging to the sides of the hills and old ruined walls and aqueducts. The prettiest sight though has been the donkeys, for as well as the old load-bearing and/or riding donkeys there have been lots of the sweetest babies, just like foals with long furry ears - sweeter than anything Walt Disney has ever drawn. *We added a baby donkey to the tortoises and the Yugoslav woolly pig in the imaginary menagerie we collected as we went along. Jim thought the truck was getting rather crowded.*

Greece seems to be a pretty backward country &, apart from the lack of monkeys in the trees, we might easily be in India. Men in fezzes and baggy breeks and women in veils ride on the donkeys. Bullocks or water buffaloes pull the carts, the houses are mud-floored and the agriculture primitive, while everybody goes armed and there are Army piquets everywhere.

The currency is getting worse and worse. We thought that 1,700 lire to the pound in Italy was high, but here we get 40,000 drachma to the pound. Nevertheless things are expensive and we are hurrying on. For instance lunch today cost us fifty-six thousand drachma and only consisted of fried fish, various chutneys and salads, a little beer and some awful hooch that tasted of liquorice.

I do not seem to have emphasised sufficiently the friendliness and kindness of the Greeks we met. During lunch a train puffed by down the middle of the street with every wagon piled high with melons. On our enquiring what sort of melons they were, someone flagged down the train and brought us one to try. It was a delicious honey melon, something we had never tasted before.

The fish and olive oil have been revisiting Jim and Shaw all afternoon, and they are sworn off Greek food now, but with any luck we shall reach the Turk frontier tomorrow. We do not yet know whether we will cross by road or rail, but trust to luck. *The Greeks and Turks were as usual making faces at each other and we were not sure whether the road would be open.*

A day or two later…

I am afraid my biro has run out on me, so I am writing on the back of a bit of carbon *paper* now.

It took us two days from Salonika to the Greek frontier, and as I mentioned, we were arrested for loitering about a bridge and spent the night in the barracks. We heard next day the reason for this. Apparently three Bulgarian saboteurs crossed the frontier the other day, loaded with bombs and guns, and everyone is on the hunt for them. So, although we were not told so officially, I rather suspect that we were mistaken for them and everyone was a little disappointed when we turned out to be just eccentric tourists.

One point I forgot to mention in Yugoslavia was that all the pigs were woolly … definitely woolly. Possibly they are bred for the bristles used in shaving brushes.

On Sunday we went on over really bad roads; so bad in fact that they were remarkable even in Greece. They were especially distinguished by the fact that all the bridges and culverts had been blown up by the partisans and consequently every time we came to a river or stream we had to ford it. This was not actually very difficult since they were all dried up in the drought. Eventually the roads got so bad that there were diversions made by the bullock carts over the countryside for miles at a time.

When we arrived at Oristias (?), quite expecting to have to put the truck on a flat car to get over the border, *(Which I rather suspect had been closed to road traffic since the Greco-Turkish war of 1921)* we ran into quite the most pleasant Customs officials and Police we have yet met. During the usual palaver we mentioned that we were thirsty, so, full of apologies, the Chief of Police took us out to a cafe and we finished the formalities over a cup of Turkish coffee.... a very small cup of coffee grounds and sugar, as it turned out. Since it was getting late, we went straight on to dinner at a cafe in the town, still with the Chief of Police, and ate kabobs and drank a wine they call Ritzina, which is a white wine mixed with resin they obtain from oak trees. Many people maintain it tastes like varnish remover, but we found it OK. *(Anyway I have never tasted varnish remover.)* During the meal another bloke turned up, who wanted to know our ranks. When told that Shaw and I were both captains, he gasped and pointed to me exclaiming "If he is a captain at nineteen, he must be like Montgomery by the time he is thirty".

Next morning after four telegrams *asking permission to enter Turkey by road rather than wait for a train,* had been sent off, the Turks replied that they would admit us; so we rattled off to the frontier. There we met a knife-rest and a Turkish post. All the soldiery in it came out and shook us by the hand. This seemed a good start but we were mistaken. Half an hour later, after a deal of telephoning, while we sat in the lorry and ate a melon the Greek Chief of Police had given us - very good, looked like jade and tasted like honey - we were allowed to go on, with an escort. He took us round to the local Army HQ, where a charming officer shared his lunch with us, then looked at our passports. We were then sent another couple of miles to the Customs. Entry into Turkey is a leisurely business and a complicated one. We were finally free of the authorities after we had visited four separate houses, drunk five cups of coffee and taken from half past ten to half past five. Not that there was any trouble or anything. While we were at the Army HQ we were shown the latest lot of Turkish refugees from Bulgaria. The Bulgars had taken everything from them before deporting them, houses, animals etc, and left them nothing but the clothes they stood up in. They were being cared for by the Red Cross, or rather Red Crescent, as it is in this country. They are coming over at the rate of about six hundred a day and are a bit of a problem.

When we stopped last night in the middle of Turkey in Europe, a vast, treeless, featureless plain, a shepherd walked up to us and presented us with a water melon. You know, in spite of these blokes not being blessed with a super-civilised welfare state, I reckon they have a lot to teach us about kindness and generosity.

Please forgive the untidy letter, Darling, as I can't see what I am writing on the back of this carbon, and in any case we have been drinking vodka for supper.

Letter 12   *The Alp Hotel, Istamboul, 19th Sept*

My darling Jane, we reached 'Stamboul this morning and have spent the afternoon getting the truck oiled and greased and seeing the Embassy, *which we found with some difficulty.*

On arrival at the Embassy we asked the Royal Marine guard for a cheap hotel, and were directed to a pension he called 'Hells Kitchen'. There was no reply at first to our bell-pulling and hammering on the large and solid door, but eventually we identified ourselves to the landlady by shouting through the keyhole, and were admitted. She was still taking no chances for she opened the door with a long piece of string on the bolt, while standing on a landing half way up the stairs, ready to escape upstairs if necessary. She was obviously very scared of intruders. This puzzled us at the time as the city seemed full of Greek shops, and the streets full of Greeks. However it was only a few years later that the Turks turned on their neighbours, who probably still formed the majority in the city, in a government organised riot, looted or burnt their shops and houses and, in a four day orgy, murdered or expelled virtually every Greek. It is now a Turkish city.

In the event we declined the proffered bedroom after one look at the unmade beds and soiled bed-linen, and found a more congenial place for the night.

This is a wonderful town..... the first we have seen with all the windows full of really good quality stuff at reasonable prices - lots of cars and taxis, no bomb damage - in fact normal. Nylons incidentally range from 10/6 for English to 25/- for American - no buyers. *Note: 10/6 meant ten shillings and sixpence. 25/- (twenty five bob) meant £1.25. However, for comparison, a captain's pay in UK was about £30 a month after tax.*

Talking of goods for sale, on the way into town we passed through the red light area by mistake. *The Turkish Police had a very simple way of dealing with congestion in the main streets. They just diverted traffic off down the side roads. Fair enough if one knew one's way about, but a trifle confusing for newcomers. Trying to get back to our route, we found ourselves in a road of rather handsome, if very rundown, Georgian houses with fine balustraded staircases leading up to the front doors.*

The popsies were all sitting at the doors *and on the staircases,* waiting for customers. Some were in jock-straps and bras, others in shorts and one in a black lace corset, very seductive! I have never seen such a collection of fat thighs in my life, not one of the tarts can have weighed less than fifteen stone and a lot must have been up in the twenty area! It was a revolting sight for twelve o'clock in the morning. *We learnt from the Royal Marine guards at the Embassy that this was known as 'Ten Piastre Street' and the girls were expecting a visiting American warship.*

Walked all round 'Stamboul looking for a Biro refill - no luck. Breakfasted off coffee and chocolate cakes, and lived on chocolate for two days. *Shades of sweet-rationing in England.* Saw the MA *(Military Attaché)* and collected dhobi *(washing).* Drank with Graves, a mad Sapper learning Russian from a General of the Imperial Guard. Very annoyed at drinking beer instead of seeing St Sophia and the old city. Sailed at about 7 o'clock *(No road bridge yet).* Long hold up at the ferry, during which someone whipped our reversing light. Drove till eleven - almost reached Ismet.

Letter 13   *On the road to Ankara, 22nd Sept*

My Darling,

We took the wrong road out of Ismet and lost four hours on what turned out to be a Turkish leg-pull. The sign post for Ankara had been pointing North instead of West for some years. We happily drove on, on a good road, until we met the sea when we should have been climbing a mountain. Lovely country - fine hills. Read the whole of Flecker's 'Hassan' out loud - sore throat - drove until after eleven. Camped about thirty miles from Ankara.

Unfortunately we are delayed by an accident, for a taxi tried to overtake us as we were approaching two other cars, all moving fairly fast on a dead straight road. The taxi could not get by in time - and should never have tried - and although Jim, who was driving pulled right over to the side and braked, the taxi ripped off its rear mudguard *(alias 'wing')* on the end of our bumper, turned a couple of circles and crashed into both the oncoming cars. Nobody was hurt and none of the cars very badly damaged, while we took no harm apart from bending one of the brackets which hold the bumper. Even the passenger in the taxi who was spilled out onto the road surrounded by bits of door and bonnet got up apparently unhurt. She must have landed on that bit of her anatomy that in Turkish ladies is very well padded.

The driver of the taxi, who looked just like Pierre Laval *(notorious Vichy French wartime collaborator)* and I then had a cursing match until everyone came up from the other cars, took our part, and tore a very large strip off 'Laval'. After about half an hour, they made him sign a chit and everyone went home.

23rd Sept, Early Christian Ruins near Guremé, about in the middle of Turkey

Fortunately, or possibly unfortunately, the crash incident was cleared up before I could finish the letter. In fact I have only just written up the second half of the account, so this is a continuation of that letter.

We pushed on into Ankara, which is a cross between Welwyn Garden City and Paris. That is two huge boulevards lined with government buildings, surrounded by open suburbs. We then stocked up with petrol, cigarettes and tinned sausages and went for a drink with some Sappers before lunch. We then went off to lunch with the Assistant Military Attaché, Col Garthwaite RA, an OW (*Old Wellingtonian*), who told us that his wife was on holiday, his cook on leave and lunch was being cooked by his washerwoman. On the way he was telling us all his woes, most of which were centred on his Vanguard (*car*). The best story was a time that after being bumped by three taxis while he was stationary, he had drawn up beside a place where the road was up. Suddenly a shovel-full of gravel came out of the hole, and broke both his headlights. He hauled the navvy out of his hole and demanded money, quite unavailingly as the bloke swore he was not paid. The Colonel was so angry at this that he seized the shovel and with a perfect golf shot holed the navvy in one, and threw the shovel in after him. Just as this story ended, the clutch rod broke and we had to finish the journey in a taxi.

Lunch was a great success and my opinion of Gunners has gone up a lot. We followed up our beer with gin, local wine and a local liqueur like Cointreau, which alone went round four times. We ended our lunch at a quarter to five and set off on our travels in a bit of a haze. However we stopped for dinner at a wayside inn and had a few more beers before finding a deserted spot and dropping into bed about sixty miles from Ankara.

We were woken in the morning by the noise of animals and bells, so were up at six o'clock and made good time all day. The roads are like corrugated iron, but not too bad. We soon passed the animals which had woken us, and got a photo of them with the truck in the background *(Like all our photos this did not come out)*, as it turned out to be a camel caravan of about thirty beasts, strung nose to tail and led by a couple of blokes on donkeys.

We had been advised *(by some American girls we had met in Ankara)* to diverge from our route a few miles and look for some early Christian dwellings, and to Jim's disapproval and Shaw's disgust, I talked them into doing so. We bumped over a lousy road for 25 miles, up and over the hills, past archaic villages and then wound down a fantastic canyon, where no lorry seemed to have been before and the limestone crags *(more probably sandstone)* almost closed overhead. Round and round we crawled with never more than a few inches to spare and not a hope of turning round, expecting at any moment to be stuck between two rocks. Shaw, by this time was making quite unrepeatable remarks about early Christians, and even Jim was swearing we would never leave our route again. Finally, half way down a precipice, we found we were there [or rather here] and set off to examine the dwellings. *Just as we came down into the wide flat sandy nullah where the dwellings are we passed a genuine troglodyte community, living in caves in the cliff wall. The mouths of the caves were hung with camel-skin curtains and above each cave there was a smoke stain from their fires. Judging from the appearance of the women and children water was not plentiful.*

The dwellings turned out to be rock holes on a fantastic scale, hewed, or should it be hewn, out of sandstone pinnacles rising out of the flat bed of the nullah *(dry water course)*. Each pinnacle contains several stories of a number of rooms, while several have the remains of chapels in them. *A feature of the chapels was that, while all the other rooms were square cut in the sandstone, their roofs were gothic arched, also in the floors of all of* them* were* graves,* cut* coffin* shaped* in* the* rock* floor* and* still* containing apparently untouched skeletons. Many of them were the* skeletons of children.*

The whole place is of course a total ruin, so many of the rooms are now open at the side, *others had neat squared windows and doors. I am sure that some of the windows and doors still incorporated decorative features like columns. The rooms were interconnected by staircases cut in the soft rock.* Nevertheless, in spite of a thousand years (or more) of rain, and the chisels of Moslem iconoclasts, the painted saints on the walls and ceilings of the chapels are still visible. The paint is bright and in many colours and the figures are done in 'stained glass window' style. *A favourite saint was George, complete with his horse and dragon.*

We have only had a quick look around by torchlight so far, but are going to spend an hour or two of exploring tomorrow. Even Jim is sufficiently worked up to want some photos now we are here. *(As I think I mentioned earlier, the rather superior camera lent us by the Army, turned out to be defective and not a single photo out of the dozens or hundreds we took came out).*

We had stumbled on the area now known as 'Capadocia' and a well known tourist site. I have no idea what the Archaeologists think of it, but I am of the opinion that it is most likely to be an Armenian settlement. In the tenth or twelfth century a large number of Armenians, fleeing the Seljuk Turkish invaders, moved into South-Eastern Turkey and established a Kingdom there. The people that lived in the rock dwellings we saw were clearly civilised town dwellers before they took to the caves. They were Christian, as were the Armenians, and one of their favourite saints was St George, who is a popular Armenian saint. Furthermore the 'Gothic' arch was developed in Armenia and only found its way to Europe during the

Crusades. I reckon these cave dwellings were the first stop of some of the Armenian fugitives.

I am afraid my letters are getting less frequent now Darling, as this is the first evening in four that we have not driven on until eleven o'clock at night, and then tumbled into bed. We are badly behind schedule as Turkey is twice as big as the War Office think. Nearly 900 miles instead of 540. *They must have got their kilometres and miles mixed up!* We are quite safe here as the girls all wear Turkish trousers.... a most ungraceful garment with the seat hanging loosely below the knees.... and cover their faces with scarves when they see us.

Letter 14   The Toros Mountains, Turkey, 24ᵗʰ Sept

My Darling Jane,

We hope to be in Allepo, or Halep as they call it, tomorrow; so I am waiting for another letter. *(care of the British Embassy).*

We spent a couple of hours in the early Christian ruins this morning and found literally hundreds of caves, many fallen in or silted up, but a lot well preserved, and more churches with elaborate 'Byzantine' painting. We continue to be amazed at the way the paint has lasted. Much of it has apparently not faded at all. The flesh tones are probably the most remarkable, though unfortunately, all the figures have been badly chipped by the Moslems.

As we were leaving, we were surprised to meet a party of late Christians in the shape of some Americans from Ankara. We had already met the girl at a party there and had an amusing few minutes. Like all Americans they were quite charming and extremely funny. Sidi had a camera, and prompted by Mama, who found our trip fascinating "I just love adventure."

she snapped everything in sight.... a Turkish cemetery, a girl on a donkey "Don't bind Momma, I'll get her!" and us "I'll call the picture 'My Three British Adventurers'", while Father, who obviously could not care less about early Christians or early anything else, just stood by and humoured the pair of them.

We made good time the rest of the day, and crossed the rest of the mountains - not as impressive as the Yugoslav ones - before we stopped for the night.

One point I forgot to mention before: - the shepherds who gave us the melon the other night wanted to know if we were 'Romany'. Shaw figured that that meant 'Gipsy'. but I thought that a bit far fetched. However it turns out he was quite right, so the shepherds must have thought us very superior gypsies in a new 2 ton truck!

Our daily routine has now quite settled down and goes something like this:-

0600 hrs ... I wake up, let down the drawbridge and put washing water and the kettle on to boil.

0615 ... Jim and Shaw get up and shave. (*I only had to shave now and again*)

0645 ... Breakfast of bread and tea with fried eggs or sausages

0715 ... Wash up, put everything away, roll down the curtains (*to keep a bit of the dust out of the back of the truck*), and prepare for the day, *while Jim does his daily check on the truck, tyres, oil, water etc.*

0745 ... Away. (*Seated three on the bench seat, and changing drivers every hour.*)

1030 ... Stop for a water melon or beer, (if available) (*It is too risky to drink water*)

1230 ... Stop for lunch and a beer

1700 ... Stop for a beer

1900 ... Stop for the night. I brush out the truck, and that means dusting everything except the roof. Shaw rolls up the curtains (*for ventilation*), Jim starts getting supper. I bath in cold water as I can't be bothered to wait for it to heat. As soon as the water is hot, Jim baths in the ally basin and Shaw in the bucket. Meanwhile we take it in turns to cook supper.

10 o'clock wash up.

1030-1130 Write up the day's run (*Letters, this journal, and the report on the roads*).

1130 ... Lights out

Letter 15　　*After Kirkuk, Iraq, Friday 29th　(I think)*

We came down from the Toros Mountains, and then along a barren and uninspiring coastal strip to Iskanderun, the old Alexandretta, tormented by the sight of the blue, cool Mediterranean on our right, but as we were all set to reach Aleppo we could not stop and bathe. *This is not as I remember it! As soon as we saw the water, we stopped, abandoned the truck at the side of the road, stripped off our dusty clothes and dashed into the water. However, this may have just been wishful thinking.*

At Iskanderun we saw the Turkish Brigade embarking for Korea in American transports. (*The Turks, with the British and Australian Brigades formed one of the United Nations divisions in the Korea War*). They are a tough crowd and may do well, but no-one knows the worth of their officers who are picked solely on social position and education. The Yanks had a lot of trouble (*A flaming row which nearly grew into an international incident*) persuading them to leave their horses (*also civilian batmen and other followers)* behind. Unfortunately it is undignified for an officer to walk even when leading an attack. *(The compromise that was reached was that the cooks, batmen, barbers, sweepers etc all came along, but the horses stayed behind. The Americans also tried to persuade the Turks that they would not need bayonets, which in modern warfare were very old hat. They were wrong. In the event the Turks fought like ... Turks.... with a distinct fondness for bayonet attacks, which the Chinese particularly feared.)*

After filling up with petrol, we pushed on and saw the lights of Aleppo as it got dark, after passing the most pleasant Customs etc we have yet met. *I dont think they can have had many visitors passing that way for some time as* We were given beer and cigarettes as we left Turkey and coffee as we entered Syria. *The Syrian Immigration Officer was particularly welcoming sending us on our way with "Enjoy yourselves, Messieurs, Our Syrian girls are wonderful!. Sad to say, being newly married, we never put his welcome to the test.*

While I was coping with the passports and Jim was handing out packets of cigarettes to quiet the Customs Officers, a civilian who was chatting to Shaw enquired how much our truck weighed. "Two tons" said Shaw. "And how many horses?" "Thirty" replied Shaw. "You know there is a road tax" We had not heard of it. "Yes there is a tax" he went on "and when they ask how much does it weigh and how many horses, you must say 'one ton' and 'twenty horses' otherwise the tax will be too big." We thanked him for his tip and were surprised to find him sitting behind the desk when we went to pay the tax! Without giving any hint that he recognised us, he asked "How much does it weigh, and how many horses...?"

We halted outside Aleppo, bathed and changed into our suits to call on the Consul, to whom we had an introduction. When we reached there we were told that he had gone on three months leave to England, but a very helpful Secretary, Mr Rickards, came out and welcomed us. Our first question of course was mail, and he very apologetically admitted that he had just sent all Shaw's to Singapore that afternoon, in accordance with Mickey's instructions on the back. He had a letter for me though.... Shaw was wild.

We then mentioned our financial problems, and he rang up a restaurant and told them to feed us and send him the bill in the morning. He also promised to change our dollars for us. As you know, Syria and Persia are not tourist countries so we have no money in them. (*Note this was a Treasury regulation, designed to save foreign exchange*). *We had filled up with petrol in Iskanderun, and proposed driving through Syria by the cheapest route, saving our few precious dollars for beer and other necessities.* When we got onto our route, however, Mr Rickards regretfully informed us that we intended to go slap through a forbidden zone at Deir ez Zor.

Next day, however, by one o'clock he had obtained permission for us to go that way, so long as we took an officer of the 'Security' with us. Meanwhile we spent the morning in the road outside the Consulate washing and maintaining the truck and doing our 'dhobi' *(Washing our clothes)*. It was a pity we had to press on, for I wanted to look round the city. The bazaar is said to cover 15 kilos of ground and to be stuffed with silks and carpets and other rare and beautiful things, while even the new city was intriguing at night with the populace all dressed in eastern robes and the sweet heavy smell of the East in the air. The most popular outfit for the Syrians seemed to be a blue and white narrow striped, long sleeved rayon nightdress, with or without a cummerbund and a white skull cap. Though there were, of course, a lot of people in Arab costume and headcloths.

We are quite in the East now, having seen our first cactus and banana tree near Iskanderun, and being quite used to the heavily loaded donkeys or the camels with their stride like a stage horse with the front and back legs almost in step, and the supercilious sneer or lecherous leer with which they look at you.

We got to Deir ez Zor with our Security Policeman, a pleasant English-speaking chap with a pistol under his coat, without trouble. When we got there we were parked in the Police Station and escorted out onto the banks of the Euphrates for a drink (for which our escort paid). The bathroom was in a hotel near the Police Station and every time one of us visited it we were tailed. The trouble was that we were suspected of trying to stir up trouble amongst the Bedouin.

Next morning we got off to an early start with a uniformed sergeant as our escort. The road had finished and we could pick our own route across a hard gravely desert, so long as we kept in sight of a line of telegraph poles. This was fine except for the chap in the back, who had to lie on my bed *(the upper bunk)*, where the air was freshest, with a handkerchief or towel over his mouth and nose. Later on we came to a road which was worse than the desert, so we followed a bullock cart track running parallel to it, only coming onto the road at the bridges. This bit was even worse for whoever was in the back, for he had to hold on with both hands to avoid being flung off the bed. Consequently my bed has now got a sag of about four inches in both longitudinal members.

The villages in this part of the country were very odd, being pimples or collections of beehives, built of mud brick and plastered in mud. Since the countryside had very little vegetation, the houses were of exactly the same shade as the land. *(which was not without interest. Somewhere we passed a 'tell', a village huddled on the top of a mound higher than it was wide. These are probably the oldest inhabited villages in the world, for the mound or 'tell' comprises the ruins of all the mud-brick houses that have gone before and may be several thousand years old. We also saw ancient caravansaries, which looked like castles, but were in fact huge fortified campsites for the camel caravans, and the ruins of ancient irrigation works. It took us a while to figure out what these were, for all that is to be seen is an apparently endless line of 'molehills' stretching from one horizon to the other, for the water channel is, or was, underground. I am sure the tell was in Syria, but the others may have been in Iraq or even Iran.*

We had left Deir ez Zor after an early breakfast and having no money (except for beer and petrol) we pushed on all day without food until we arrived at the *(Syrian/Iraq)* frontier at about seven *o'clock, after thirteen hours driving.* There our curmudgeon of an escort left us without giving us so much as a cup of coffee, while we waited at the railway station customs office for the authorities to clear a passenger train. An hour and a half later we got our exit stamps and entry into Iraq settled, and also the Syrian Customs, but a pot-bellied little Iraqi told us that his customs house was in Mosul and we should have to go straight there. We explained that we wanted to sleep on the way, but he was adamant and made us take a policeman with us to make sure we came straight through. We asked about the road and he said it was a good tar road, the policeman knew it and we would do it in two and a half hours.

So we swallowed our hunger and pushed on, determined to feed in Mosul.......... The road was worse than the one we had left. The Policeman, *who admitted that he only knew the way by train,* had not been along it for two years and led us up to an impassable river, *which we crossed by driving over the railway bridge, bumping over the sleepers and hoping a train did not come along,* and it was nearer one hundred miles than the seventy we were told. We arrived in Mosul, which is the most stinking city which we have yet met, at a quarter to one *in the morning.* 'Could we break off?' - 'Not blooming likely!'. We had to (*take the truck and*) go and turn out the Customs Officer (*at home, which turned out to be in a block of flats built around a courtyard, with balconies on the inside, in the depth of the city*) who, (*turned out in his pyjamas, up on the balcony, intimated that the Policeman was an idiot and*) told us to go away until nine next morning. *We returned to the Police Station and* at a quarter to two at last settled down, cooked our second meal of the day and went to bed cursing all Iraqis and especially the pot-bellied little .... and blessing Robin Barton (*married to our cousin Kim Frith*) who had given us a bottle of brandy for medicinal purposes.

We had got half way to Calcutta

Part Three: Mosul to the Afghan Border

Letter 16   written from somewhere beyond Kirkuk,
Iraq, 29ᵗʰ Sept 1950 continued

The city of Mosul is the dirtiest in the Middle East and the noisiest at night. The dogs bark, the jackals howl, the cows moo, the policemen whistle to keep themselves awake, the cocks crow all night and even the donkeys have the loudest and most musical bray in the world. And if the noise stops for one moment the smell gets worse.

(The problem is the watchmen employed by every shopkeeper. To prove that they are awake, every now and again one blows his whistle, the man outside the next shop takes it up and passes it on until every whistle in the bazaar is blown. This starts the dogs, which starts the jackals, which starts the cocks and the donkeys and the cows and finally the camels...... and as soon as the hullabaloo dies down, some idiot blows his whistle. If you want a quiet night's sleep do not camp in the middle of the Mosul bazaar, as we were forced to)

We settled the Customs in the morning and visited the Consul, who greeted us royally with mail, beer and the offer of a bath, which we accepted, *(He also upbraided us for not coming last night, but agreed that we might perhaps have been less welcome* at *three o'clock in the morning!)* lunched us and sped us on our way to Kirkuk, with an invitation to spend the night in the Consulate garden there, and an introduction to his wife.

Mrs Sinclair was even more charming than he, giving us another bath, more beer, a lovely supper and insisting we slept the night in the house. She must have had a trying evening for a mad surgeon and his doctor wife also dropped in for the night. She was on her own, he having to run both consulates.

This morning we had tea in bed, a shower before breakfast and left the breakfast room at ten! Mrs Sinclair inveigled the Bank Manager into cashing our cheques although it is a holiday here today, and put us in touch with the Iraq Petroleum Company's set up here, whose workshops checked over our shock-absorbers. *(They also sold us petrol at the Company's internal price ..... 1½d per gallon of which ½d was tax. It smelt horrid, but we filled all our spare jerrycans, which were in a rack under Jim's bed, and lived with the smell).* We spent the rest of the morning mending the lock on her front door and after lunch pressed on.

The Kurds round here are a ferocious and romantic looking lot with their coloured siren suits *(a siren suit was the war-time precursor of the track suit, very suitable for donning in a hurry when the air raid sirens woke you in the middle of the night)*, bright sashes, turned up toes and embroidered skull caps wrapped around with a large loose-fringed turban.

Kirkuk is an extraordinary sight if you approach it, as we did, by dark. The road, which had been excellent all day, runs over undulating hills of barren sand, eroded into craggy gulches and sandy slopes. *While still a long way away* we started to notice the light of the fires in the sky. *Soon the sand hills were pitch black on our side and bright pink on the far side. As we approached Kirkuk, the glim resolved into* three bright orange glows illuminating the horizon; *eventually becoming three* brilliant *lights. We watched* one of the lights *rising gently until, to our amazement, we saw it* lift bodily into the sky. It was the moon. However, at last we crossed the last hill and saw the fantastic panorama. Half a dozen pipes rose out of the ground and spewed flame at the sky *(nobody had thought of selling the gas in those days).* A welter of lights lit up the aluminium painted tanks *and* silver towers topped with red lights. Drilling rigs like the pylons at Blackpool thrust up out of the darkness, while behind lay the lights of the town, and before, the howling wilderness of sand.

(Correction: My apologies for the purple prose. The sandy hills were not howling, just parti-coloured black and crimson.)

Letter 17   The Aid to Russia Road, Persia, 30ᵗʰ Sept

My Darling Jane

After writing last night to say we were all in good health, the scene has changed and Jim and Shaw have both got tummy trouble. They put it down to the fact that beer is hard to get and they have to drink water. It has taken the form of a craving for drink. Breakfast this morning was tea, lunch Sherbet, a kind of oriental orangeade, at tea time we had some beer and when it came to supper they said they wanted nothing but Bovril. I complained, so they agreed to have a second course of cocoa as well. I am glad to say that I am OK though and have demolished most of a packet of Vita-wheat with honey.

The landscape has changed spectacularly in the last hour or two. After running all day over flat desert, with or without a road, only relieved by the odd oasis or little sandy hills, soon after we entered Persia along the grand tarmac road built during the war to push supplies up to Russia, the country changed and we have been winding our way up through craggy gorges and broken mountains with streams and rivers in all the valleys.

Iran

I ate a pomegranate today for the first time.....
disappointing.... it looks like an apple, its rind is like an
orange and it is full of a million pips each surrounded by a
bitter-sweet pulp. A complete waste of time to eat, though I
think that pomegranate juice and gin would make an excellent
drink.

Letter 18   *Almost Teheran, Persia, 2nd Oct*

Darling Jane,

I have had bad luck with the mail; first of all we missed the
last town with a post box in Iraq, so my letter no 15 never got
posted, and then yesterday was a public holiday in Persia, so
16 and 17 never got sent off. However we should get a Post
Office in Teheran tomorrow OK and of course there will be a
letter from you!

We have been up in the high ground ever since entering
Persia. *(I must apologise for using the name Persia, but people had
not yet got use to the name Iran. Indeed, when we asked for the
names of all the countries we intended traversing to be painted on
the side of the truck, we were surprised to find that the list included
both Iran, which we had put in, and Persia which the signwriter
thought we had left out).*

The scenery today, though, has not been up to that of the last
two. Yesterday we drove over a marvellous pass, with
smooth barren hills hemming in a narrow valley and the road
climbing in and out up one face. It was evening and the sky
was stormy, all scarlet and green, while the hills are of red
earth or purple with copper green streaks and splashes. It
would have made a lovely picture but was too dark to
photograph. It has got chilly too up here and after sleeping

almost naked in Iraq, we have been shivering under a couple of blankets here.

The people are not nearly as colourful here as they were in Syria and Iraq. As in Turkey there has been an attempt to modernise the place, with the result that everyone walks around in cast-off rags of second-hand European clothes. Some of the old women though look very striking in long robes and shawls with a dark turban and long noses and black eyes peering between dark locks of hair - just like witches.

Some of the roads have been almost as bad as those in Greece. What is most annoying is that it has been a first class tarmac road and through lack of maintenance it has gone into potholes. The repair organisation is most erratic, for miles the potholes get worse and then you meet a gang filling them with gravel, *(which is quite useless as the traffic just throws it out again)* while, a mile or two on, you come to first class tarred patching, almost as good as new. But this will not last for long, and soon you are on to a mile or two more of gravel or another ten miles of holes.

Jim and Shaw are better, which is a great relief, for we are starting to feed again. I think it is the prospect of diplomatic beer tomorrow that has put their tummies right.

Shaw, after saying the other day that he would never need to use his hands again when climbing or descending ladders has just fallen head-first in at the door with a jerrycan in one hand and the basin and soap in the other! *(He must have bounced as he was not injured).*

Saw three gazelle today - lovely.

Letter 19   *The Park Hotel, Teheran, 3ʳᵈ Oct*

My Darling,

We met a fascinating character today called Haigh. C. Gulstain, the local Austin Agent *(See photograph at front page)* After spending the night just outside Teheran - on a lovely campsite that Shaw swore was the worst we had ever struck because there was no culvert *(we could use as a loo)* - and being woken again by the music of camel bells, we reached the city at about nine o'clock and soon found the shop. We were greeted by a pleasant Englishman called John Dickson and an Irani, Prince Adoub, who took the truck to be washed and greased and sent our laundry round the corner. After we had seen the Military Attaché and the Consul, we went back to the shop and there was the Agent himself - a heavy man of about forty-five with greying hair. He asked us if we were fixed up and then told his entire staff, two or three times, that we were to be his guests. Just then his phone rang, but instead of answering it, he unplugged it and, calling in his Secretary, Rubina, a handsome Persian girl, he gave her the phone to take away. The whole time he was talking to us he punctuated the conversation by shouting instructions down an inter-office communications set. The whole place was well set up, with a large staff, but they did not seem to sell any Austins, and in the garage too, out of twenty or thirty cars and trucks, there were only two or three Austins. The whole set-up looks very phoney, but whether it is a cover for opium, politics or what, we cannot guess.

Nevertheless he gave us a smashing lunch of borsch, ravioli and fried turkey and rice washed down with a very fine wine from Shiraz. It is said to be the original sherry - and I have seldom tasted better. *(We were introduced to a singular way of drinking our wine. You drink half the glass and then top it up with ice-cold mineral water, drink half again and top it up again, and again until you are drinking pure water. It is then time to fill another glass and start again. This was not a bad system for a hot climate.)*

After lunch we went back to the office, where we were interviewed by the local reporter. This was a priceless affair. After writing down our names – there was a difference of opinion over Shaw's name of course. They insisted on calling him Shah, until we pointed out that it was the same as George Bernard Shaw. "Ah, George Bernard Shove, I read all his plays." was the reply. (*'McCloghry' they found equally difficult .... and as far as I can remember he ended as Shove Mac-coolie-ghary).* Incidentally, when we protested about being written down as Mr, we were told it was safer! After we had given a list of the countries we had been through, Haigh took over. For ten solid minutes, without reference to us, he told the reporter how good the Austin was. Later we went off to the Garage to take photos, the prize one of which is the front of the truck poking out of his gate, which is covered with painted advertisements for himself and Austin. (See back cover)

Letter 20   Still in Iran, 6th Oct

Darling Jane,

We had been praising our Dunlop tyres, which up to then had given no trouble at all, not one puncture and no wear on the treads, and asked if there was a Dunlop agent in the town... Soon we noticed Haigh printing something on a slip of paper. After a lot of chatter with the reporter he handed him the slip..... which read HENLEY, for which Haigh is the agent!

We spent the night in the best hotel in town (as Haigh's guests) - only £5 per person per night - We also had a huge dinner and signed for it, but we had a fit of conscience when it came to paying for our drinks for we sat listening to a first class band until about midnight. However while we were arguing with the waiter, the Manager arrived and was most indignant - on no account were we to pay - He had strict instructions that we were to be Mr Gulstain's guests. (*I wonder whether Haigh owned the hotel.*)

Next morning we collected our laundry (£3-10-0) at the office and were then trotted off to the War Office, where the truck was inspected by a large number of officers of varying rank, until at last we saw the Second in Command of the Persian Army. We had a most amusing interview. He spoke a bit of English and was most interested in the performance of the lorry and the trip. "A very interesting journey" he commented "with one eye for yourself and one for your Army"! *He had rumbled us.*

After a bit more chatter, he came and looked at the truck. While Shaw and I explained its good points, Jim snapped him as he looked under the bonnet. That was just what Haigh wanted. The old General knew his stuff though, and questioned us pretty thoroughly on our spares (*none of which we had used*) and any trouble we had had, and made us promise to send him a report when we had finished. I feel that what Haigh was after was a socking great Army contract. However he stood us another lunch and filled our tanks, and did not even charge for the maintenance or the laundry. We worked it out that that piece of advertising must have cost him nearly £30.

While I chose a piece of Persian silver (price eight shillings) as a memento, (*It was a pretty little bracelet, with painted miniatures in it)* and sat drinking Vodka and lime in the hotel, Jim and Shaw went off to the Afghan Embassy, where they were greeted as lost brothers by the First Secretary, who had been in England all the war. They were champing to be gone and aching for a drink, while this bloke reminisced about Manchester, Cornwall and Southampton. "I love the English." "I'm Irish" says Shaw. "Ah Captain Macooligharry, I love the Irish and the Scotch too. I have seen Liverpool." Eventually he got down to writing out a 'visa' for the truck, tore it up, wrote another, amended it, and wrote a third, all in longhand pothooks. Jim and Shaw turned up an hour later, having forgotten who it was they had to give it to.

We have been driving over corrugated roads ever since. Pitch one foot, depth of corrugation three inches. And as the soldiery would say we are proper browned off with Persia. There are only two possible speeds, 40 mph and 15 mph, and we are only making about 150 miles a day. *(At 40 you ride over the bumps but wear out your springs and shock absorbers. At 15 you just wear out your temper).*

We saw two more gazelle today in the desert.

The Gazelle is a pretty creature,
with a little white behind.
In the desert, that's a feature,
and the 'he' gazelle you'll find
will spot her and will reach her,
though he is miles and miles behind.

(I think we composed the poem as we went along).

We stopped in a village for supper, and had fourteen eggs and three yards of bootleather. The eggs were fried with tomatoes and onions, and the bootleather was a kind of chapatie a yard long and a foot wide and much the same shape as half a gumboot cut lengthways. They had been baked on hot stones and still had pebbles sticking to them. However it was a good meal as we had had *just* bootleather and water for lunch.

We have had two spots of bad luck with the truck. Yesterday a shackle bolt came out of one of the back springs and carved a groove ½ an inch deep all round the inside of the tyre before ripping open the inner tube, and today another tyre got badly gashed by an unidentified hazard, so we are without a spare wheel. It is bad luck that our first two punctures should each write off an outer tyre.

Letter 21   *Islam Qala, Afghanistan, 9ᵗʰ Oct*

My Darling Jane,

We have at last reached Afghanistan (*Islam Qala, formerly Kaffir Qala, the fort of the infidels, is the frontier town*), and swept the dust of Persia out of the truck. We have never been so glad to leave a country. The last few day's driving have been deadly dull. Pottering along over medium bad roads at 20 miles an hour for ten or twelve hours a day (*Our schedule was 200 miles per day*) over a flat dusty, featureless plateau on a dead straight road.

We are still laughing about our water supply at Teheran. Haigh told us that the best water in the town was at the British Embassy, so there we went to find a spring of fresh water that looked remarkably like a drain. In fact it seemed to wander round from one house to another, being used for any purpose on the way. It was full of vegetation in some places and ran under some very questionable buildings, while it was used for washing clothes or watering the garden in other places. Finally it fed the swimming bath. The story goes that it is then sold to a firm of mineral water bottlers. We asked one of the Secretaries whether or not it was drinkable. He replied that it was said to be, but he, personally, always drank mineral water!

A feature of Teheran is the silence. No horns may be blown in any town. The penalty is ninety days goal, and, as Haigh said, "You cannot buy it."

I posted my last letter at an out of the way town called Sabziwar, the day before we got to Meshed. We drove into it as far as we could go and then Jim and I went on, on foot, to find the Post Office. Finally we came on another main street with fine big brick built shops (instead of mud) selling wares from Birmingham, Bombay and all spots between. The only thing missing was a Post Office. We asked several times for the 'Posty-Telegraph' and at last a small boy led us through a labyrinth of narrow passages to a little door. On the other side we found a fine courtyard with the Post Office on the far side. I handed my letter through a grill and the Clerk looked at it upside down for about five minutes and then said 'Russia?'. Eventually another bloke turned up who realised we wanted 'Englistan', and then Jim, just to make sure gave his celebrated imitation that serves for a chicken or an aeroplane. Then the 'book of words' was produced and read - I think for the first time, because they left a thumbprint on every page and there were none there before. Finally 'Englistan by Hawai' (which I hope meant 'By Airmail') was found and he stuck three stamps on the back of the letter.

We hoped to make Meshed that night, and pushed on. At last we got to the end of a range of hills we were skirting and turned North East, so I confidently predicted that it would be twenty miles more or at the very outside thirty. After going twenty we hoped to see the lights of the city over each rise – not a hope. Finally, when we had gone fifty eight miles, we packed up for the night, having decided that it was too late to see the Consul anyway. Next morning Shaw and I had a really good wash up of all our kitchen gear, much to the surprise of a couple of beggars, whom we called Abdul and Ali (after Flecker's characters), who obviously did not see the object. However they retrieved a foot or so of week-old bootleather we had thrown away and sat there chewing. The only thing they managed to steal was the padlock from the ladder (*The ladder, which served as our front door steps, was stowed crosswise under the truck and retained with a padlock.*) and as this had been giving us trouble we did not object. We have a couple spare. *(Whether it was this day or another I cannot remember, but I nearly caused an accident by forgetting to secure the ladder properly. We noticed oncoming vehicles giving us a wider and wider berth, until Jim stopped the truck, looked out and noticed the ladder sticking out about six feet horizontally into the oncoming lane.)*

We then drove off to see the Consul General, Mr Dyke, who was most charming. He found out the local rate for tyres (£60 a pair!) *(This was clearly outrageously expensive)* rang up to find where we could get tins of petrol as there is none to be had in Afghanistan since Pakistan cut off supplies and finally gave us a welcome beer in his lovely garden and then an excellent lunch. We decided that there was life in the British yet for the last party to come that way had been an Englishman, his wife and three young children on an old motorbike and sidecar.

They were emigrating to Australia and had got tired of waiting for a ship!

Meanwhile we had taken our tyre round to a small shop to be mended if possible, as we could not possibly *afford to* buy a new one. The shopkeeper turned up his nose at the one that was almost in half - but gave us a pound for it - but said he could do the other. His method of patching was to strip the tread off an old tyre, and cut out a segment of canvas about two feet long, which he sewed inside our tyre. The fact that both inner tyres had six inch slashes in them did not worry him either and he pointed out a lovely eighteen inch patch he had just finished working. The old man was obviously the boss, but all the work was done by a boy of about eight, and even when two other birds helped assemble the wheel, it was the boy who showed them how, even seizing their tools and doing a bit himself if they were more than ordinarily inept. *(I have no idea what I meant by 'birds', I am sure they must have been male!)*

After picking up our tyre, we pushed on and reached Farimun at about half past six. We located a tiny chae-khana where they brought out a carpet for us to sit on and then asked, in Persian, what we wanted. The first thing that appeared was tea, so Jim again gave his imitation, this time in the hope of eggs or chicken. At long last the bloke said 'soup'. We assented vigorously and, not knowing what to expect, got a yard or two of chapatti and three bowls of excellent mutton or camel broth...... first class.

We filled up, today, at Tubot i Sheik Jain, and when we asked where we could *buy* food, we were taken off to the shopkeepers' house. Here we washed our hands in the goldfish pond in the middle of the courtyard, and sat in his drawing room, a lovely cool room with mud walls and domed

Iran

roof three feet thick. He served us himself, but we had no language in common, so conversation was limited.. First of all tea with the glasses held in little silver bowls, then two kinds of melon, then more tea, and finally the 'piece de resistance' seven fried eggs, tomatoes and chips, served with spring onion leaves, mint sprigs, chutney and cherry jam, not forgetting a liberal supply of boot leather. *Although she must have prepared this feast for us, we never saw our host's wife, and were unable to thank her for this singular and generous hospitality.*

We had a very slow time at the Customs this evening. In Persia everyone was asleep, or couldn't read, or did not know the ropes and we took hours. This was a considerable contrast to the Afghan Customs Officer, who was the most efficient bloke we have yet met. Despite letting Shaw sit at his official desk, while he squatted on the carpet and wrote on the floor, and licking the passports before putting on the rubber stamp, he got through our papers quicker than anyone since Dunkirk.

Part Four: Afghanistan, Pakistan and India

Girishk in Afghanistan,
                              12th October

My Darling Jane,

After crossing the Afghan frontier, where we had to ford a very broad, but very shallow, river because half the fine old bridge had been washed away, we passed through Islam Khala, a typical Afghan town, single story flat-roofed houses huddled together, with a busy bazaar where we had to thread our way through crowds of people, livestock and camels. It may have been there that I noticed that the stalls in the bazaar were set between a double row of vast columns, much higher than the buildings. We concluded that we were driving up the nave of a temple dating back to Alexander the Great's day.

We rather like Afghanistan so far, though it is not at all as we imagined it. In the first place we have seen no mountains, worthy of the name, and at one point today there was not even a hill in sight, just desert as flat as a parade ground as far as the eye could see in all directions. Usually there have been a fair number of craggy hills rising sheerly out of the desert, and sometimes we have had to climb over little ranges. The desert was at first more fertile than the Persian desert, with quite a lot of camel thorn bushes and a bit of grass here and there, but today we have been passing a pretty arid area, and, apart from the oases, where streams flowed and the land was cultivated, we have been travelling across either black or ochre desert with hardly a thorn to relieve it. The black desert was rather impressive for the hills were black too, and altogether it had a grand and eyri (or is it eeri, eery or eary?) atmosphere - it was so big.

The other unexpected feature of the country is that no-one carries arms and there is no banditry. Even the police and army are virtually unarmed, unlike any other country we have passed through. In fact everyone has been almost embarrassingly friendly. Especially embarrassing at night when everyone drops in for a chat whatever the hour. I suppose it is so unusual to see a lorry at all, that one parked at the side of the roads is worth investigating. However we draw the line at being woken up and keep silent until they go away. Unfortunately they are a persistent race and a couple of blokes spent from three o'clock until half past the other night shouting "telephone to Teheran" varied with "Khalifa" at us and then tried serenading us in Afghan. We were just about ready to get up and knock them on the head when they went away. I don't think they were drunk either for we have not been able to locate any liquor at all yet in this country. *(If my memory serves me correctly we were rather more worried by this incident than this letter suggests. We had stopped in the middle of the desert and had not expected anyone to find us. I remember lying very still in my bunk with a dagger in my hand in case they tried to break in).*

But not to worry. We have now stopped sleeping in the wagon and are availing ourselves of a first class chain of hotels that are situated every seventy miles or so along the road. They are very cheap and appear to be run by the Government. They are quite new and clean, usually well furnished and with lovely carpets, and the food is good. Admittedly, not all the very up to date sanitary equipment has water laid on. However it is nice to sit in a chair and write at a table again. They only charge about 25/- *(£1.25)* a night, with dinner and breakfast all in, for the three of us.

The roads have not been bad. They only consist of tracks across the desert, but the surface is hard and smooth, which is a nice change after Persia. Petrol too is very short and we hardly meet more than two or three vehicles all day. Herat was remarkable for having more traffic police than motor vehicles. It is a large town, the second in the country and has suffered from an excess of *town* planning. Besides the old town, built by Alexander the Pig, and the Bazaar area, there is a new garden city with all the houses set in lovely parks and all the roads double track boulevards. At every crossroads there is a traffic cop waiting to wave on any traffic that comes his way. But we only saw one Jeep, half a dozen lorries or buses and half a dozen pony traps, besides a few camels.

One result of the petrol shortage we saw this evening. About twenty miles out of Girishk we met a bus (that is a lorry holding about fifty people and their kit, in two layers, one on the roof) broken down at the side of the road. The passengers blocked the road and stopped us, and then offered to buy petrol from us, as their bus had none. This was a bit embarrassing as we have only about enough to see ourselves through *to Pakistan* – for we have no ration and the black market is expensive – and we had to plead we were nearly empty. After a bit of chatter, we agreed to take one bloke on to Girishk to get some. So we chased off all those clinging to the sides, and squeezing a greybeard into the cab set off. We could not, of course, let them see in the back, where all our jerry cans were full and neatly stacked and labelled against the side. When we had got out of sight we stopped for me to get in the back. To our considerable surprise another bloke appeared who had been travelling on our petrol tank. I hopped in the back and slammed the door in his face, and he very sorrowfully went and interviewed Jim, who made him ride on a wing for about ten miles. This 'larned' him sufficiently, and he came and rode in the cab, getting back his spirits by taking large mouthfuls of opium.

It is lucky we have chosen the dry weather, for most of the bridges are down and we have to ford the rivers. Usually there is no water.

An extraordinary feature of the population here is the amount of clothes they wear. While we are quite happy all day with a cotton shirt and drill shorts and sandals, they wear thick shirt, a thick waistcoat, a heavy overcoat and a bit of cloth over the shoulders for luck. The theory may be to keep the sun out.

The letter I posted in Herat cost 4/6d (*about 25p, which may not seem a lot until you remember my salary was not much over £1 per day*), which so shocked Jim and Shaw that this one may have to wait until we get to Kabul in two days time.

Letter 23   *Hotel de Kaboul, Ghazni, 14th Oct*

Darling Jane,

We are about eighty miles south of Kabul now and hope to reach it tomorrow morning. We tried to post our last letters at Kandahar, but unfortunately, being a Friday, the Post Office was shut. So this one will go with the last at Kabul. We still have not much of an opinion of the Afghan scenery, it has been quite flat all the way so far, either desert or ploughed land, though there have been hills in the distance on both sides. However the people we have met have been quite interesting. For some reason everyone seems to be travelling the other way from us, for all day long we have met caravans of nomads, complete with their gear and children on camels and donkeys, and small flocks of sheep and goats in attendance. The men are a good looking lot with long beards and coats and noses, while the women are unveiled and uniformly ugly, though loaded with silver jewellery. Great forehead decorations and huge necklaces as big as breastplates seem to be the fashion, though a few wear nose ornaments. The men still seem to us to be vastly overdressed, though I suppose this is because the nights are getting very cold, and they do not bother to take the stuff off in the middle of the day.

We were quite surprised at the cold until we found that our maps were contoured in metres, so we are now at well over seven thousand feet, not two thousand, *as we had supposed.*

We were a pretty odd looking lot when we got up this morning, for it was bitterly cold in the truck. I had been up first and piled on more and more clothes until I was wearing a sweater over my camel skin coat lining, blue cords over my shorts and my old songkok (*a Malayan cap*). Shaw was a pile of sweaters and Jim was draped in blankets.

This evening we have just met a marvellous bloke who looked like a bear turned inside out. You could only see his astrakhan hat and head poking out of an enormous coat. We talked to him for a long time about the First War (*1914-18*) when he was in the Russian army, and the time he was a trader buying silks in Japan and trading them for caviar in Harbin, - and all the time admiring his coat. Eventually Jim traded him his trench-coat, (*a sort of mac favoured by sleazy stage detectives*) sports jacket and daks (*a popular brand of grey flannel trousers*) for this marvellous garment. It is three and a half yards round the bottom, two yards long, four feet across the shoulders and the sleeves are two foot six long. It is made of unclipped goat skin, each piece cut especially from the backbone. It had been specially ordered for this bloke and he had just taken delivery after waiting three and a half months. He swears there is not another as big in Afghanistan. Now Jim looks and smells like a flock of goats turned inside out!

I must try and get a smaller edition tomorrow. *(which I did, and very useful my 'poshteen' has been, although people I shared a tent with on winter nights up to five years later have been known to observe that it was like sleeping with a herd of unwashed goats!)*

Letter 23   *Kabul, 16ᵗʰ Oct*

My Darling Jane,

The other thing I forgot to mention in my last letter was a memorable meal we had at Ghazni. It consisted of chicken soup and a huge plate of rice - about 24 oz I should say - with two chickens, one roast and one boiled. We were very hungry and cold and fell to ravenously, but I am afraid Shaw hadn't much of an appetite. He could only manage as much rice as he could pile on his plate and half a chicken. Jim and I upheld the honour of the party, though I must admit we left one leg of chicken! Now we are all in hospital.

We left Ghazni about half past eight with quite a load in the back. Our trader friend of the night before, an army officer and a fine looking bloke they called the Khan as well as a couple of hangers on - my uncle and my cousin - and a pile of kit. Their bus had broken an axle and they had sat half the previous night out in the cold and then been held up for a day, so they were very pleased when we gave them a lift, and the forty nine other people on the bus, who had stayed by it instead of coming back to the hotel, were correspondingly angry when we refused to take the whole lot. However they treated the Khan with considerable deference, so we had a powerful protector.

We arrived in Kabul about two o'clock, after travelling through country that begins to look like our idea of Afghanistan, narrow valleys and rocky hills, but nothing very rugged yet, to find that Teheran had warned the people here of our arrival and everyone was waiting for us. They even had a ward of the hospital ready as sleeping quarters for us, and entertained us last night.

Today we have got to raise some petrol, get our exit visas and see Abdul. *(An Afghan Army Officer friend we had known in England while on a year-long course at the Royal School of Military Engineering.)* Shaw has already gone for the mail. Then we push on to the Khyber.

Letter 24   *Still in Kabul, 18th Oct*

My Darling,

We are all fit, and have spent a couple of infuriatingly idle days, lazing about, *drinking the First Secretary's beer* and overeating. I have been getting more and more impatient, but Jim and Shaw have loved it. The hold-up has been due to the usual oriental slowness in dealing with our exit visas; however we will be on our way this afternoon, stage the night at Jalalabad and reach Peshawar tomorrow.

Meanwhile, although we have been very well looked after here, sleeping in *(what I think must have been the embassy)* hospital, and spending the days with Mr Philips, one of the First Secretaries, and his family. We have seen the ambassador etc, but we are really very annoyed that we have

63

not been able to get in touch with Abdul. I am quite sure he is in the town, but it is out of the question to try and contact him except through official channels, because the Police would be straight on to him if we tried. In Kabul itself the Police are very suspicious of foreigners, and consequently the *Afghan* War Office has regretted that they are unable to trace him. It makes me furious. *We should, however, have guessed the situation when the people we had given a lift to scuttled off like rabbits when we arrived in Kabul, lest they be seen talking to foreigners.*

Kabul was a pleasant town. I do not remember any modern buildings, but there was a hundred yards of tarmac road, the first we had seen since Teheran, outside the Russian Embassy. The Russians had also built several kilometres of a new road heading eastwards. We were told it was a pleasant place for a picnic, much favoured by the people of Kabul. So one day Mrs Philips sent us off with a pack-lunch and a warning not to go too far. This we heeded, for without warning the road finished on the edge of a precipice! Where the Russians thought they were going to, I cannot imagine.

Letter 25 was all personal stuff and not copied into my journal.

Letter 26   *from Agra, India, 27th Oct*

My Darling Jane,

To pick up the thread of my story, I will have to go a long way back. We left Kabul in the afternoon and pushed on to Jalalabad the same night. Although we crossed an eight thousand foot pass, the scenery was not really much to look at, just bare sandy hills, until we came to the gorge of the Kabul River after Serobi, then we had a breath-taking ride in the dusk between huge walls of stone, *which towered above us until there was hardly room for the moon to shine between them,* with the road stuck on the edge hanging over the river *far below*, or popping in and out of little tunnels. It was grand.

(We were driving even more carefully than usual, for the Embassy had warned us that in the event of any accident with a camel, or any other animal, the driver would be held to blame and have to reimburse the owner of the beast. In the event of a human death the life of the driver was in the hands of the victim's relations who could demand a life for a life or settle for blood money. The driver of one of the Embassy cars had frightened a camel on this same road. The camel bolted, lost its footing and fell into the gorge. Unfortunately there was an infant strapped onto its load. The car driver had to escape to Pakistan to save his life.)

Next morning we left the hotel at Jalalabad quite early and pushed on, climbing steadily over the usual second-class road up to the Khyber.

The Pass itself was heralded by a few tiny forts sitting on the tops of quite impossible pinnacles, and then a heap of old oil drums. These were scattered at random over a flat piece of ground, and at first we merely wondered why a couple of dozen scrap 800 gall drums should be there, but soon we realised that it was the stock-pile system the Afghans have devised to beat the Pakistan petrol trouble. The row is due to the fact that the Pakistanis will not allow the old Afghan wagons, which are merely three-tonners with a tank on the back, into the petrol depot. They maintain, quite rightly, that they are dangerous *(fire hazard)*. They gave the Afghans six months to get some new lorries or modify the old ones. Naturally, the Afghans did nothing – so when the time limit expired, there was no petrol for Afghanistan. Their reaction to this was to spend a couple of months getting one tanker modified, and then run a shuttle service over the frontier, with this selection of stray tanks as a staging point, and their own antiquated vehicles filling up there and going round the country.

(As I suspect that all the pumping was done by hand this must have been a slow business, so it is not surprising that there was a petrol famine in Afghanistan).

In contrast to the Pakistanis, who occupy the improbable forts, that can only be reached by helicopter or mountain goats, *(and I do not believe the Pakistan Air Force had any helicopters then)* we found the entire official staff of the Afghan Border *Post, Customs Officers, Border Guards, Passport Officers* etc asleep, with their heads and all rolled up in sheets. Finally we found one bloke awake and when we showed him our passports, he pulled the big toe of another pile of bedding and produced the Passport Officer. He obligingly licked and stamped our passports and we set off for India.

(He licked the passports before stamping them because his ink pad was as dry as a bone. There was enough dry ink on the stamp, however, to produce a workable impression if dampened).

In a few yards we might have been in another world. The road became a lovely smooth tarmac, the officials were all awake, the Khyber Rifles were beautifully turned out in rifle green berets and starched KD *(Khaki Drill uniforms)*. There was even a railway as far as the frontier.

Instead of jolting along, the truck sailed smoothly down the road, winding in and out of some of the grandest scenery we have seen. The hills were bare rock and topped with forts all the way; the road and rail and two other old roads formed a criss-cross pattern all down the Pass, and at intervals we came to massive concrete tank obstacles. *(Many of the cliffs were decorated with huge painted carvings of the cap-badges of British regiments who had served here in the days of the Raj).*

I remember one glorious moment when we stopped to admire a vista of the plains below; miles upon thousands of miles of bright green wheat fields; a pleasant change from the sand and desert of the Middle East. The hills got less and less steep until we came to Fort Jamrud, which is a massive round tower surrounded by concentric rings of battlements, *standing like a sentry at the gate to India.* Now at last we were down on the plains and on the last lap of our journey, only a thousand and a half miles to go!

Still revelling in our lovely road, we pushed on to Peshawar, confident that if Shaw hadn't hit anything on the way down, he was likely to miss everything on the flat. *(This seems a grossly unfair comment. Shaw's driving was certainly no worse than mine, and it was probably the combination of the two that gave Jim an ulcer; but read on).* Remember we had just come down a hill section with a fast surface, and the rule of the road is to drive on the left; the first time in the lorry, *since we had left Dover,.* Shaw's driving merited our confidence and we got in to Peshawar, without a hitch, in time for tea.

As soon as we were fixed up in the Club for the night, we rang up Fazl-i-Khaliq in Charsadda, about ten or fifteen miles away. *(He was the Father of Fazl-i-Raziq, a Pathan officer who had been on the same course as Shaw and I at Bangalore, been commissioned on the same day, and with whom we had been in communication before the trip).* He was very glad to hear from us and said that he had left a message for us at Tor Khan on the Frontier, which had not been delivered, but in any case if we cared to come out in two days time he had a shikar *(hunting)* party laid on in the tribal territories for General Jamieson and he would be delighted if we would join it. After a long conference we had to decline the offer though on the grounds that we could not hope to reach Calcutta in time if we spent four days at Peshawar. It was a pity that, as the chance is not likely to recur.

Next morning we spent looking at lovely carpets and Kashmir shawls; one that I thought you might like as a birthday present was only £15 *(half my monthly salary)*, so I decided it would be just the job for your 73rd birthday. I am sure you will appreciate a Kashmir Shawl much more then than now. *(By coincidence we were back in India fifty years later and I did buy Jane a Kashmir Shawl, and paid a lot more than £15!)*

I also spent an hour or two in the Bazaar, for, having missed Aleppo, I could hardly face Sandy *(Jane's uncle)* if I did not look around Peshawar, which is the least spoiled of any mid Asian city and has a fame spread far and wide. All the trade with Afghanistan and the Middle East, as well as the trickle that remains with Mongol Russia and Kashmir, pass through the city, which is a smoking hubble-bubble of wonder and delight, though sufficiently odiferous to gladden the heart of even such a collector of malodorous stenches as Sandy. To be quite honest though, the smell was compounded of sweat and spices rather than inferior drainage, although the tanneries did knock one down a bit.

As regards the architecture of the place, one can only assume that most of the houses started as bungalows and have grown upwards in process of time, like trees after sun and air. This has the effect of making them start as mud at the bottom, but turn into a jumble of crazy wooden skyscrapers, leaning drunkenly towards each other or out over the street. The streets themselves were obviously fitted in between the houses after they were built. They zigzag and wiggle, widen and narrow and now and again go up flights of steps. The narrowest places are, of course, the most popular for extra stalls, barrows and beggars, for one is bound to look at their wares *or sores*.

There is an opening or square in the middle, but apart from a few vendors of iced water and sugar cane, it is reserved for the elite of the bazaar, the venerable patriarchs who sit cross legged on their string beds and write letters for you, the money changers on their splendid carpets with piles of notes and coinage of every country round them and a hawk-eyed warrior bristling with guns and swords just behind, and the money-lenders too, fat men dripping with goodwill and the lust for money, squatting in a pool of flesh on their carpets and only too anxious – on sufficient security – to lend you money at 75% *interest* per year.

Men from all the ends of the world gather to haggle and trade in the bazaar, but mostly it was the grey astrakhan caps of the Afghans and the tall pugris of the proud, fair skinned Pathans that mixed with the darker peoples of the plains, amongst whom every trader bore the mark of his penury or prosperity in the size of his belly.

The goods too were as varied as the vendors, sweets or corn cobs cooked on a brazier on the pavement were on sale next to shops full of silks from the East or cottons from the South. A stall full of cages of hawks and singing birds was next to a shop full of exquisite Kashmiri carving. Lovely silk embroidery on the back of shaggy goat skins, was flanked by cheap Birmingham tinware and a teashop called the Grand Hotel. Women in white boorkhas, looking like walking laundry bags edged their way through the bright yellow painted tongas *(horse drawn cabs with two seats facing forwards and two backwards)*, whose drivers, had the road been wide enough, would have kept their poor beasts at a gallop all the time. Gleaming brassware and astrakhan caps, Bata shoes and Sheffield steel, English bicycles with Japanese bells and always the strong heavy sweet smell of spices, sandalwood and incense made up the sights and smells of this queen among bazaars.

Our route now lay straight down the Grand Trunk Road, built by the Mogul Emperors, but took us via the Officers Mess of my Father's old regiment, the 4th/13th Frontier Force Rifles, and the King George the Fifth Military Memorial Schools, which he had founded after the first World War, as well as through the hospitable hands of the Royal Pakistan and Royal Indian Engineers. Our debt to these officers is deep, some few expected us, some we already knew, but many received us on the slightest of introductions. We were highly impressed, not only with the good fellowship of the officers, but with the magnificent bearing and smart turn-out of the troops.

We came to appreciate the realities of the partition of India on Independence when we crossed the heavily armed Pakistan/India frontier between Lahore, a city where nowadays no Sikh is seen, and Amritsar, aswarm with the hirsute race.

This next letter was to my Father, who had spent most of his working life as an officer in the old Indian Army up on the North West Frontier, hence the emphasis on military matters.

Calcutta

Letter 27

5 November

Dear Dad

It was an absolute delight leaving Afghanistan for Pakistan. For the first time in weeks we were riding on a smooth nicely graded tarmac road, quite different to the bumpy tracks we had been driving over before. It was also nice to see some properly dressed soldiers again, as all the armies since Italy had been clad in dirty overalls. However the Khyber Rifles came up to the mark and it would have been difficult to pick any faults in their turnout, KD and rifle green berets.

The Frontier is quiet at the moment. I fancy the tribes had their belly-full of fighting in Kashmir, and the pass was not very strongly held, though some of the forts and pillboxes were manned and there are a lot of wire and concrete obstacles, left over from the German invasion scare of the last war.

It was delightful after Fort Jamrud to get back onto a fertile plain and see some growing crops again instead of the empty desert we had got used to all over the Middle East. May we never see it again!

We spent the night in the Peshawar Club, which is hardly altered at all... There is no nonsense about prohibition up on the Frontier, although down in the Punjab you have to have a medical certificate and coupons to cope with... (When I returned to Pakistan the next

71

year I had to register as a drink addict with a ration, which I hasten to add I never used, of 12 bottles of whisky a month!)

While in Peshawar we got in touch with Fazl-i-Khaliq the AC at Charsadda, whose son we know well, and the old man promptly invited us to join a shikar and fishing party he was organising in the next few days. It was a lovely opportunity, but we had to turn it down as we could not afford to spend three days there.

(The War Office had allowed us exactly 28 days travelling time plus our annual leave in which to reach Singapore, after which we would go on unpaid leave and lose seniority, a serious matter and good reason for pushing on.)

So with many misgivings we pushed on to 'Pindi (*Rawalpindi*) *where after failing to contact the EinC (General Veitch, Engineer in Chief of the Pakistan Army)*, we paid a call on the 4th/13th.Frontier Force Rifles (Wilde's Rifles) (*My Father's and Grandfather's Regiment*). They were a trifle surprised at our turning up in the evening, but soon rallied around and produced beer and baths for us, insisting that we dine with them and stay the night. Conversation was a trifle strained at first, although they were undoubtedly very glad to know that old officers of the regiment were still taking an interest in them, and after they had discussed for a long while whether such and such a sweeper had known you, or whether such and such a Subedar might have been a lance-naik in your day, I was getting a little bored and threw a bombshell into the conversation by asking what they had been doing in Kashmir.

This had exactly the effect I hoped for, for they at once dropped the lance-naiks and sweepers (whom you had probably forgotten anyway) and got onto the much more interesting subject of the present state and recent history of the

Regiment. All the senior officers of the battalion, down to the Adjutant, served with the battalion during the '39-45' war and are steeped in and immensely proud of its traditions and military history, and they are quickly beating the youngsters into shape. At the moment they are having an all out battle to retain their distinctive equipment and blue facings *(awarded them for gallantry in the Indian Mutiny)*. In view of the number of senior Piffers in the army I feel that they will win.

The exploits they seemed most proud of recently were two battles for hills in Kashmir. In the first one, the battalion pushed a Sikh brigade off the top, and in the second, one company of the 4th/13th put in a frontal attack on a company of Gurkhas and made them run. They were very pleased with this as the Gurkhas still have a fine reputation. The Company Commander is waiting for the King to approve his MC. *(Pakistan was still a Commonwealth country)*. They are convinced that they are still the finest regiment in the army and that they could wallop the Indians whenever they chose.

The reasons for the Pakistan stand in Kashmir are two. Firstly the head-works of vast agricultural irrigation works are there and if the Indians in Kashmir chose they could waste the water and turn the Punjab into a desert, and secondly, strategically, an Indian army in Kashmir is round the end of their frontier and a constant menace to Lahore and 'Pindi.

After we had bathed and changed we went over to the Mess, which they share with the PAVO *(Prince Albert Victor's own Cavalry)*. It is not really big enough, but nicely got up with some fine old weapons on the walls over the photographs, and a lot of silver out on the dining table. Unfortunately, you had jumped off the wall the week before and needed a new glass, but Grandfather's *whiskers frowned down at us during dinner, in company with all the other COs since Wilde himself.*

It was amusing to find your's or Grandfather's name on many of the cups and trophies. One, which I recognised at once was the Chinese Junk – a very fine model *which had been presented in memory of the Regiment's service in China during the Boxer Rebellion. Grandfather was commanding at the time, and we had a miniature of the junk at home.* Also, to see you in old group photos of football and polo teams. A lot of Grandfather's sketches were up on the wall too.

After dinner, just in case we were still under the impression that you had left no mark behind, they produced the photo albums and went through picking out first your Father and then you. I think it was the first time that Jim or I had seen a photo of Grandmother! We also saw pictures of Gordon, *(Ronnie Gordon, killed on a Frontier campaign, after whom I am named)* Trail, and all the others of your contemporaries that you tell stories about. Then we came on to the new albums and saw the Regiment in Kashmir.

Altogether it was a memorable evening and I think you will be glad to know that the regimental spirit and tradition has not been affected in the least by the change over of Pakistan to Dominion status and the loss of the British officers. They are all most anxious to keep in touch with old friends.

The morning after our party with the Piffers and PAVO Cavalry we went down to GHQ to present our letter of introduction to the Engineer-in-Chief. He was out when we arrived but our friend from 16 Supplementary Course (at the Royal School of Military Engineering in Chatham), Lt Col Humayune-ud-Din, looked after us and pressed us to stay the day. We excused ourselves on the grounds that we were behind schedule, but this availed us nothing when the General came in and said it was out of the question for us to leave before lunch. He was most interested in the trip and thought it a first class effort. In fact, he was so interested that he took us round to all the other staff officers, including the Commander-in-Chief and introduced us. I think we had a cup of tea with every one above the rank of colonel in GHQ.

As we were walking between two of the offices the Engineer-in-Chief said he was looking for officers like us and wished we would stay. (The Pakistan Army, at that time, had plenty of excellent infantry and cavalry officers, but were very short of Gunners, Sappers and other technical officers, most of whom had gone to the new Indian Army on the partition of India two years before.). He followed this up by calling in his Staff Captain and telling him to get out the list of vacant majorities. There were three: Two Field Company Commanders and a Roads Instructor at the SME (School of Military Engineering). He then turned to us and asked if we wanted them with the pay and rank of majors. *(This was a very attractive offer to Shaw and me, as we could not hope for promotion to major in the British army for another five or six years at least, and the command of a Field Company was our dream).*

My first thought of course was of Jane *(My wife of four months)* and I put off giving an answer until we got to Sialkot where a friend of ours Lt Col Bob Lindsell is an instructor at the SME. I knew his wife well and wanted her opinion. *(It was Pam Lindsell who, in Bangalore in '46, mistook my Christian name and referred to me as 'Iain' when talking to Bob. He called me 'Iain' and, as I was too shy to correct him, I have been Iain ever since).* Later, when we reached Sialkot, the red carpet was out for us again. Pam and Bob both reckoned it was a good thing and Shaw and I both put in for it. *(Volunteered for secondment to the Pakistan army. The War Office in London allowed me to return about six months late, but had other ideas for Shaw)* But more of this later, we are still in 'Pindi.

After our morning at GHQ, we went on to lunch at the Sapper Mess with Col Humayune, who gave us much beer and wished us God-speed on our way to Jhelum.

We arrived at Jhelum over a fantastically long bridge just as dusk was falling and stopped at a spot called the King George's Military Memorial School (of which you may have heard), *(My Father, of course, knew it well. After the first World War, in which thousands of Indian soldiers in the (British) Indian Army died, a considerable sum of money was collected for a war memorial. A competition was held for suggestions as to how this should be used, and my Father suggested that it be spent on a school for the sons of Indian soldiers. This plan was adopted and he was given the job of starting it and appointed the first Commandant. He planned and built the school and got it going so successfully that a second school was authorised at Jallundar, which he also commanded. Just after he left the schools he met the Indian Civil Service officer in charge of all education in the Punjab, who praised them as the two best schools in the province and wished he had more like them. Jim, I think, was born there).*

We were entertained by the Commandant in his bungalow that evening, and looked around the school the following day. It is rather a lovely spot with the sweep of the buildings softened by the trees *(which Dad had planted)* with gardens at the front and playing fields behind. *(When the buildings were complete, a finance officer from GHQ congratulated Dad on completing the work well within his budget, and observed that the balance of the funds collected would go elsewhere, only to be told that every last rupee had been spent on the grounds and playing fields.*

The one thing that Dad had no money left for was a 'mango top' or orchard. He wanted to give the boys a source of fresh fruit. However he persuaded every fond parent who visited the school to present one tree as a memorial to his son, and, by the time he left, the 'mango top', to his great satisfaction, was flourishing. I did not dare mention in the letter that, seeing no 'top', I queried its absence, to be told that a previous commandant had fought a long battle with the finance department, who maintained that as the trees were growing on government ground the produce was government property and the boys could only have the mangos as part of their rations. The Commandant lost the battle and had the 'mango top' cut down. When I returned to England several years later Dad enquired after the 'top'. His reaction to the story was "Quite right. Exactly what I would have done!")

Unfortunately it was a holiday so we did not see the boys at work, but were taken round by the Senior Under Officer, or whatever they call the Head Boy. There have been considerable additions to the school since your day; a new science block, a new house, and a swimming pool are probably the main ones. There have been changes too to the type and object of the education. Although the intake of boys is exactly the same as before *(except that in Jhelum they are all Muslims, while at Jallundar they are Sikhs and Hindus, instead of being mixed)* they are definitely being regarded as potential officers and so long as they pass their 'Special Exam' they are eligible for selection for the Military Academy. Those few who fail, of course go into the ranks of their father's regiments. We met a selection of the boys of all ages on the Commandant's lawn in the afternoon and were struck with the intelligence of the boys, their keenness and their interest in and knowledge of world affairs. For instance I spent a long time discussing devaluation, which had recently struck our Labour Government, with a fourteen year old. If these are the next generation of Pakistani officers, their army has little to worry about.

Other disjointed points I noted were that the grounds were well looked after and the trees, gardens and playing fields much appreciated. The record of the School both scholastically and in sports is very good, and the boys look fit, proud and very smart. Incidentally, they all want to go in the Tank Corps.

We went on from Jhelum to Sialkot where we were greeted with open arms and bottles by the SME (School of Military Engineering). Bob and Pam Lindsell *(Colonel Lindsell had been my first commanding officer in Bangalore)* assured us that Pakistan was a good spot. Actually they found that their money was short, but they were buying a new car! We checked on pay and quarters and everything seemed to fit, so when the Commandant started his private recruiting drive by showing us right round the SME, Shaw and I more or less signed on. We were promised an answer by the 1st of November which would allow me time to alter Jane's passage from Singapore, *to which it was already booked*, to Karachi).

Next day we pushed on across country just recovering from terrific floods, which have affected the Punjab. The road *(which is carried on an embankment above the expected level of flooding)* had been swept away in a hundred places and squads of Sappers *(Royal Pakistan Engineers)* and gangs of coolies were busy putting up temporary bridges and making diversions. The Army all say that the PWD (Public Works Department) would have been helpless without the Sappers. We spent the night with a British Officer who is CRE *(Commander Royal Engineers)* of the Lahore Division. *(My Father went to France with the Lahore Division in the First World War)*. He entertained us well and took us to the club. This, I think is the last club in Pakistan or India which will not admit non-Europeans. Consequently the members were an awful collection of third rate Englishmen who would never have got into any club a few years ago.

We found a copy of Winnie the Pooh in our bedroom, and read it, much to the amusement of our hostess, before going to bed.

Our journey from now on was a constant worry about the Pakistan show. We had been promised word, *of whether the War Office in London would agree to our secondment to the Pakistan Army*, at a number of places, and dashed from one to the next hoping for a telegram. There was no word here.

We crossed the Frontier next day between Lahore and Amritsar. This was about the most militarised frontier we came across, with very smart, khaki drill clad, Punjabi Mussalman *(the old name for Moslem soldiers)* eyeing equally smart Sikh soldiers dressed in jungle green. The Indians also wore distinctive pugris (turbans) or berets;. the Sikhs in scarlet pugris, the Hindus in scarlet berets; very smart, but a bit odd to our eyes. We thought at first that they must be Military Police, but it turned out that this was the normal kit for the Indian Army Infantry. Arms and Services have now all got their own coloured berets, for instance Sappers, blue and boys, leaf green.

We did a very successful smuggling act across the frontier. We deliberately left the car papers in the truck, and while we cleared our passports and customs papers we made friends with the Sikh officer who did the job. In the middle we were disappointed to find that he remembered and asked for the truck papers, so I went and got them, but when I came back with them in my pocket, I found everyone chatting about the world in general and everything except the papers.

Eventually we had a cup of tea and parted the best of friends with the papers still in my pocket and the truck smuggled through with no customs paid at all. *In the event this turned out to be a very expensive mistake. We were trying to be too clever by half, for, when we tried to sell the truck in Calcutta, we could not prove that it had been legally imported.*

We stopped at Amritsar to change a cheque and bashed on to Jallundar with all possible speed. There we descended on the Commandant of the King George's Memorial School at an impossible time of the evening and quite put the poor man out. However he gave us baths and invited us over to a boxing match being staged at the school. It was however just a Command *(or military district)* Finals and had nothing to do with the boys. However we at once met a couple of officers we knew from a Madras Sappers and Miners Field Company. One of them, Captain Vijay Rama Rao, had been at the OTS (Officer Training School in Bangalore) five years previously with Shaw and me, so we were old friends. Jim also met several Sappers who had served under him in the past, and I got news of several of my 'old' men.

Of course we were carried off to the Mess for more drinks than was good for us and were promised a really good Madras curry the following day. We had been looking forward to this ever since we left the fleshpots of France. We came back to the Commandant's house later than we had said we would and made a very hazy effort to eat and be sociable. Shaw collapsed, or rather dropped off to sleep, first and we were glad of the excuse to go to bed.

Next day we asked the long-suffering Commandant to show us the School but were rather disappointed. The buildings and grounds were still in good order and on the surface all seemed well, but the atmosphere was not the same as at

Jhelum in Pakistan. The Commandant told us that the civil authorities were doing their best to elbow in on the Army's control by threatening to stop the money, and it was only a matter of time before they tried to take over. Of course, the Army in India is suffering at the hands of the 'babus' *(an impolite term for clerks or civil servants)*, whereas in Pakistan it is the mainstay of the country. The sort of trouble they are having is that the civil education people are trying to cut out the military training. They have already said that boys need not go into the Armed Services when they finish at the school, and the Army fear that the next step will be a demand for vacancies for boys not from army families.

Whereas in fifty years time the school at Jhelum will be the 'Pakistan Junior Military Academy', I fear that the other will be the 'Jallundar High School for Boys and Girls'. Nevertheless, however gloomy the future, the school is still working now as intended, and the Commandant (a Jat) is more of a soldier than his Pakistani opposite number. The boys are still smart, intelligent and sons of soldiers. They do well at games and exams, but, instead of wanting to be Tank Corps officers, they all want to go into Ordnance or IEME *(Indian Electrical and Mechanical Engineers)*. We met your old dhobi (washerman), sweeper and Art Master, who have all spent their lives at the School – and all send their salaams.

The next stop in our triumphal progress was Delhi. There we drove into GHQ and promptly met another officer who had been at the OTS with us, Captain Y.V. Rama Rao. *(who, in Bangalore, decided that I needed educating, and had taken me into a restaurant in the city and insisted on my learning to eat curry and rice with the fingers of my right hand. Getting my fingers (up to the elbow) in a rather wet curry had proved a mildly traumatic experience for a nicely brought up English boy, but I soon got the hang of it!).* We were soon in the presence of General Williams, the Engineer in Chief, who regretted that he was too busy to entertain us but lent us his own car and told his Personal Assistant to show us the town, put us up in his own rooms at the Club, and rang up the Manager to see that we were fed and looked after! Still a little shattered by this hospitality, and wondering whether he too wanted to recruit us, we drove around in his luxurious bus and saw Humayune's tomb, the Red Fort and the other sights of the town.

That night we dined in the grillroom of the club, as we had no dinner jackets. We were in luck as they had managed to smuggle in some steaks – strictly illegal in a beef-worshipping country – and had a very fine dinner. They had recently let an artist loose in the room and the Members were a bit self conscious about the huge murals which portrayed fat jolly devils cooking and serving beautiful maidens!

Next day we went into the town proper and, to Jim and Shaw's disgust, I spent all our available cash on a lovely Kashmir shawl for Jane. It is of soft ibex wool, about four foot square with an embroidered border.

We pushed on with only money for petrol in our pockets and spent the night in the MES (Military Engineering Services) bungalow in Agra, where after a good curry we went to see the Taj Mahal by moonlight. It is much lovelier than its pictures and still in perfect condition, unlike all the other tombs we had seen which had been sacked by Jats, Maharattas or the British. The Taj, however is a miracle of design, so simple in its lines, so beautifully finished to the smallest detail, whether it be a mosaic of semi-precious stones or a screen of carved marble. It is a jewel enlarged.

I think this was the one bit of sightseeing Jim and Shaw didn't regret. *Had we stopped to examine everything I would have liked, we would still have been somewhere in the Middle East by this time. However I still regret not having taken in the Hagia Sophia and the Golden Temple in Amritsar!*

We then drove hell for leather *(bearing in mind that Jim never allowed us to exceed forty miles per hour lest we waste petrol)* down the Grand Trunk Road determined to reach Calcutta by November the First, to keep up with our itinerary, and got there in two days, two nights and a morning of driving, only stopping for five hours sleep on the way. We had one disappointment though, for the railway bridge over some river or other, whose name I have forgotten (the Pun possibly), was closed to road traffic, and, *because we were late arriving*, instead of getting straight over on a train, we were told we could wait all day or take a diversion half way round Bihar State. We were so impatient that we did this. If we had only made the train we would have saved a hundred miles or more.

Nevertheless eventually we got to Calcutta, through miles and miles of the most revolting slums *(Huge numbers of Hindu refugees from what is now Bangladesh had settled there after the division of India at Independence)* and called on Mr Ganguli *(The Austin Agent)* in Chowringhi Road. There we found no word from either 'Pindi or Austin. In fact Ganguli had little idea of who we were, apart from a letter from Wilde *(the Austin Agent from whom we had bought the truck)*, and obviously was not much interested. He was, however both polite and helpful and got us fixed up in a Quaker hotel, where most people appeared to us to be slightly mad, though very nice. *(I wonder what they thought of us!)*

After a couple of days avoiding prayer meetings though, we contacted the Gurkha Transit Centre Mess at Barrackpur and shifted our base there. They looked after us well, but I am afraid I spoilt the party by throwing a dead faint in the Mess, (on nothing stronger than nimbu-pani *(lime juice)*, and retiring to bed with jaundice.

Our two major worries about this time were whether or not we were going to Pakistan – remember General Veitch *(the Engineer in Chief, Pakistan)* had promised us an answer by November the First, and we had given him Ganguli's address. This was of course mostly my worry, as I had to confirm Jane's passage to Singapore *or change her destination to Karachi,* and how we were to get down to Singapore. For several days we wandered around the incredibly filthy and beggar-strewn streets of the town, checking on boats, calling on Ganguli to see if there was a cable for us. By mutual consent, Shaw and I left the sale of the truck to Jim.

We seemed to draw a complete blank. The last boat had sailed a couple of days previously and there was not another for a month, so, as my *paid* leave was running out, I did a spot of arithmetic and decided an air-passage was cheaper than losing my pay and paying the boat fare. Also I *was not at all well and* was scared of landing in a Calcutta hospital. The Assistant-Surgeon, having tested me for malaria, VD and alcoholic poisoning *had declared me fit, but* was bound to notice my colour sometime, so I went off wearing dark glasses *to disguise the fact I was bright yellow,* and booked a BOAC passage *to Singapore* on the last day of my leave. After a very pleasant flight, during which I had to keep on my glasses while being violently 'air-sick' at the same time, at last we arrived at the loveliest of Eastern cities, where the Army took charge of me.

When they learnt I spoke Malay, they sent me straight on to Hong Kong. I am starting a correspondence course in Eskimo in the hope I may get sent back to Malaya again someday!

Although I was going by air again this time, the only resemblance *to my flight from Calcutta to Singapore* was the unearthly hour they expected one to parade on the airstrip. I feel there must be an international convention that prevents planes taking off in daylight. This time, instead of a Quantas plane with billowy armchairs that reminded me of a super dentistry with no drill and beautiful hostesses to bring one refreshment, we had an old Australian Air Force Dakota with a canvas bench against the wall, *(the side of the plane's hold)* and, when we had been flying for about five hours, someone mentioned that breakfast might be a good idea, we were told by the co-pilot that there was a box of sandwiches and some cold tea in the back, and we could help ourselves. Luckily I have a unique capability of sleeping on any occasion and it came in useful then.

We landed at Saigon on the way up, and it was very odd hearing what looked like Malay waiters speaking pidgin French instead of English.

To my intense surprise, I was met at the airfield by a subaltern of the Squadron *I was joining,* and treated with considerable respect for a day or two. It turned out that they had looked up the RE List, to find out who I was, and took me for Jim, thereby adding 5 years to my seniority *and taking me for the new OC.*

So for me the Trip was over. Shaw came up later in a Philippino cargo boat and Jim, as usual, fell on his feet and carried out our original plan of a year ago of coming up free with the Gurkhas *by getting himself appointed the Draft Conducting Officer for the next party of Gurkhas returning from leave.*

The only outstanding hazard is the sale of the Austin which is still in Calcutta. If we do not lose too much on that we shall have broken about even financially. Petrol cost us exactly £100 *(from Calais to Calcutta)*, food, beer and living generally another £100 and we had to pay *Shaw's and my* fares to Singapore and various bills before leaving home *(which amounted to another £100)*. Against that we *each* drew two months pay and allowances *(about £60 after tax)* and £42.10 passage money.

The Austin had done a thousand miles a week for eight weeks with the failure of one bolt in the springs, two punctures, a little trouble with a shock absorber and the sump drain plug coming loose, and this over the worst roads in the world *and* with two bad drivers. *(By the time we got to Calcutta, perhaps we had improved. I hope Jim would have agreed!).* Well done Austin!

I think I can fairly say that all the extra fittings we had put in the truck were used and useful, except the fire-extinguisher! Our vast weight of spares for the truck, however were never even unpacked *until we sold them to Mr Ganguli*. I think we used one rear light bulb out of the whole lot.

The ration stores, however, were a great asset, for though we might have got by living off the land, it would have cost us a lot more of our precious 'Tourist Allowance' *(The Government limit on how much foreign exchange one could spend on holiday)* and infinitely complicated our cooking, As it was we usually contrived to have our main meal of the day at 'Tiffin' in a café or 'chaekhana', thereby sampling the local diet. Our breakfast and supper, however, were normally eaten at some spot well away from villages or towns and then we supplemented our local supplies from the ration locker.

On the whole the supplies were what we needed and lasted very well….. for instance, I think we had about one tin of veg left when we got to Calcutta, and the only things we had to restock were *tinned* sausages and milk, of which we got a resupply from NAAFI in Ankara. Some things we had too much of though. Of tea and coffee, though we each drank three or four pints a day, we had a large surplus. One of the most useful items was the supply of Vita-Wheat. It served as bread much better than biscuits did. Incidentally we badly overestimated the amount of soap we should need and had a lot over.

So on the whole you see Mum did us very well for stores..

Finis

Posted in
Hong Kong
Nov '50

Jim followed me to Hong Kong, where he was given command of a Gurkha Field Squadron RE. Shaw was posted to a British Field Spuadron on Malaya. Jane joined me in Hong Kong, where Joanna was born, and in due course, I returned to Pakistan on secondment to the Royal Pakistan Engineers.